# Sailing Directions

# Granite Sea

# Granite Sea

## Navigating the United States Navy Memorial and Visitors Center

To Helene —
an ode to
immortality —
Love you
Arena

**Thomas Coldwell**

*Captain, U.S. Navy (Ret.)*

Published by the United States Navy Memorial Foundation. Profits from the sale of this book will be used to defray the cost of operation and maintenance of the Memorial and Visitors Center.

Library of Congress Card Number 92-064054
ISBN 0-9619812-1-0
Printed in the United States of America

First Edition

*Book Design*
    Ernest McIver

*Printing and Color Separations*
    Stephenson Printing

Cover: Lone Sailor statue © Stanley Bleifeld

William Thompson
*Rear Admiral, U. S. Navy, (Ret.)*

WILLIAM THOMPSON, president and chief executive officer of the U. S. Navy Memorial Foundation, enlisted in the Navy in 1942 and was commissioned in 1945. He served in the Korean War as Operations Officer in a destroyer. For more than half his Navy career, Thompson served in public affairs assignments including Special Assistant to three Secretaries of the Navy, Deputy Chief of Information and finally Chief of Information for the Navy Department. He was the first public affairs specialist to be selected for flag rank in any service.

Upon retiring as a Rear Admiral in 1975, Thompson received the Navy's Distinguished Service Medal for "creation of the most effective and professional public affairs program in the history of the United States Navy."

Admiral Thompson became actively involved in the U. S. Navy Memorial Foundation in 1978 and became its president in 1980. In recognition of his work on the Navy Memorial—culminating in the Memorial's dedication on October 13, 1987—Thompson received the Navy's highest civilian award, the Distinguished Public Service Award, from the Secretary of the Navy.

Thompson holds a degree in political science from The George Washington University and has pursued graduate studies at the University of Missouri, Harvard Business School and the Naval War College. Originally from Green Bay, Wisconsin, he and his wife Dorothy reside in McLean, Virginia.

# Welcome Aboard!

WELCOME TO THE U. S. NAVY MEMORIAL—whether you are making your visit in person or solely through this book, the founders of the Navy Memorial and the crew are pleased to have you aboard.

What you see in these pages and at the Memorial here in Washington is the culmination of more than 14 years' work on the part of the U. S. Navy Memorial Foundation, its distinguished board of directors, a loyal and dedicated staff of true professionals, and a small army—no, *navy*—of volunteers, most of them wives of present and former Navy men.

As you will learn in these pages, the Navy Memorial story goes back farther than 14 years, back to the very foundations of the nation's capital. The Navy Memorial is new, but it is rich in tradition and heritage that parallel the history of the Navy and the history of the United States.

It has been my privilege to have been at the helm during the long and arduous voyage that brings us to the realization of an important Memorial and tribute to the people of the Navy. Here on the bridge have strode our chairmen and honorary chairmen, whose leadership, vision and strong support have been the inspiration and key to our success.

If you have been able to visit the Navy Memorial now that its construction is complete, I say welcome, thanks for your visit and come back soon. If you have not, I urge you to visit soon. And if you are among the more than a quarter-million present or former members of the Navy family or its friends or corporate supporters who have contributed to the building of this Memorial, I extend to you warmest thanks for your help and congratulations on a job WELL DONE!

William Thompson
*Rear Admiral, U. S. Navy (Ret.)*
*President, U. S. Navy Memorial Foundation*

# Setting the Watch

THE UNITED STATES NAVY MEMORIAL honors all men and women who serve in the United States Navy—past, present and future.

The Memorial recognizes those who went down to the sea or served ashore, the warriors and the watchstanders, the people who waited in lines and the ones who formed them, the battle veterans and those who yearned for the call. From 1775 to the present and beyond, regular and reservist, wartime conscript and volunteer, retired and mustered out, fleet admiral to boot seaman—all are commemorated in this Memorial on Pennsylvania Avenue, halfway between The White House and The Capitol.

Designers placed highest priority on creating a living Memorial, a Memorial which would contribute to the culture and environment of the city and help bring people back to Pennsylvania Avenue, in keeping with the spectacular redevelopment of America's Main Street.

Visitors today step from this avenue into a nautical world, past a bronze compass rose and through an entrance flanked by fountains and waterfalls and on to a 100-foot diameter plaza bearing the largest map of the world. Colored granite inlays set off sea and land areas of the world, showing the U. S. for what it is, a virtual island nation, dependent largely on its Navy and the people the Memorial honors. The huge grid serves as an amphitheater for outdoor concerts by the U. S. Navy Band and other service bands performing on a four-tiered stage located on the circle's northern edge. Fountains and raised waterfalls surround the grid map, their pools "salted" by water samples from all the world's oceans and the Great Lakes.

A permanent presence among the tourists and lunch hour sun-seekers on the world grid is one of the Memorial's most imposing attractions: the seven-foot tall Lone Sailor statue, strong and resolute in his endless vigil for his country while ever longing for his home. The Lone Sailor represents all who have served or will serve. He is the classic American sailor.

The Memorial also displays heavy bronze relief sculptures depicting events in Navy history or recognizing communities of the Navy.

The Memorial's Visitors Center includes a motion picture theater, Presidents Room, Ship's Store and the Navy Memorial Log Room.

The dream of a Navy memorial here dates from the 18th century, when architect Pierre L'Enfant laid out his magnificent plan for the nation's capital. As will be seen in the pages to follow, there have been other dreamers as well.

From a two-century old idea through modern concept, design, funding and construction, the U. S. Navy Memorial is now a reality—a fitting tribute to those who have served America on the frontiers of the sea.

Paul N. Howell
*Rear Admiral, USNR (Ret.)*
*Chairman of the Board of Directors*

· · · · · · · · · · · · · · · · · · · · · · · · ·

*Energy industrialist, engineer, combat veteran and retired Naval Reserve flag officer, author, civic leader, husband and father, Paul Neilson Howell was elected in February 1989 to be the Chairman of the Board of the Navy Memorial Foundation. The Memorial's top official is chairman of the Board and Chief Executive Officer of the Howell Corporation, an energy industry holding company which Howell founded in 1955. A naval officer in World War II and the Korean War, Howell rose to the rank of Rear Admiral in the Naval Reserve. He was in USS Neosho at Pearl Harbor and a survivor when the ship was sunk in the Battle of Coral Sea. He joined the Memorial's board in 1986.*

· · · · · · · · · · · · · · · · · · · · · · · · ·

# Charting the Course

Master Chief Hospital Corpsman Jay Hood, U.S. Navy (Ret.), raises the colors at the Memorial. He serves as the Master Chief of the Navy Memorial.

GRANITE SEA, the story of the U. S. Navy Memorial and the Visitors Center, is named for the 100-foot diameter map of the world which forms the main plaza of the Memorial. While cruising through these pages, the reader will observe all the major elements of the Memorial and learn how and why they all came together to form this national tribute to the men and women of the Navy.

All the parts of the Memorial and the Visitors Center are present in these pages but not their sum, the actual experience of visiting and immersing one's self in America's great naval heritage. Although confined to words and pictures, this guide is a start, an effort that is—unlike the Memorial which is always awaiting new glories of naval service—a finished product. To that end I sincerely thank Rear Admiral Bill Thompson for his inspiration, patience and editorial counsel. I extend thanks also to his staff (my good friends and co-workers, whose names are listed later on); to the bronze relief sponsoring organizations, Captain Robert S. Jones and Leo Irrera for resource material on the bronze relief program; to all the photographers whose works are credited in the back; to Ernest McIver for designing this guide; and to my best friend and "First Mate" Mary Ann Coldwell for her support and encouragement.

—TC

From the beginning . . .

# United States Navy Memorial

## Crown Jewel of America's Main Street, Pennsylvania Avenue

## Fulfilling Different Dreams for Different People

**W**ashington is the town where people bring their dreams to make them come true. They may call their dreams "agendas" or "programs," but they're dreams all right. Typically, some dreams conflict, but more typically they attach themselves to one another, unrelated except in combination as their best chance of coming true.

The U. S. Navy Memorial is a product of such unconnected dreams—unconnected as to time, space, purpose or the dreamers themselves. Somehow they got connected and came true.

The first dreamer was architect Pierre L'Enfant, whose plans for the nation's capital included a column "to celebrate the first rise of the Navy and consecrate its progress and achievements."

The second dreamer was President John F. Kennedy, a Navy veteran, who inspired the establishment of the Pennsylvania Avenue Development Corporation

to restore the Avenue to a stature befitting "Main Street, U. S. A."

The third dreamer was Admiral Arleigh A. Burke, World War II war hero and former three-term Chief of Naval Operations, who, in the Spring of 1977, declared, "We have talked long enough about a Navy Memorial and it's time we did something about it."

Those are the three dreams, apparently all that was necessary for the Navy Memorial. Except for the work.

Others listened to Admiral Burke, including Admiral Thomas H. Moorer, another former CNO and Chairman of the Joint Chiefs of Staff, and then-current CNO Admiral James L. Holloway III.

Admiral Arleigh Burke, USN (Ret.)

"Midway between the White House and the Capitol. . ." Arrow marks location of the Navy Memorial. The large white area at lower right is a light reflection of the Tidal Basin. The photo was taken on Flag Day, June 14, 1991; a large American flag , 411 feet in length, appears on the Washington Monument grounds.  Aerial photo courtesy of Air Survey Corporation, Sterling, Virginia.

THE UNITED STATES NAVY MEMORIAL

IN HONOR OF THOSE WHO SERVED TO FORGE THE
HERITAGE OF THE UNITED STATES NAVY

IN TRIBUTE TO THOSE WHO PERISHED TO PROVIDE PEACE
AND SECURITY FOR OUR MARITIME NATION

IN GRATITUDE TO THOSE NOW SERVING

Located at the entrance to the Memorial, the compass rose recalls one of the earliest and still-used navigational instruments, with the cardinal and intercardinal points surrounding the Navy Seal.

The U. S. Navy took up the matter then referred it to private sector friends of the Navy, Navy retirees and Naval Reservists wearing their civilian hats to establish, in 1977, the private, non-profit U. S. Navy Memorial Foundation.

In 1980, under the presidency of Rear Admiral William Thompson, USN (Ret.), the Foundation undertook a drive to achieve five objectives necessary in the building of a memorial in Washington: enabling legislation, design, site selection, fund raising and construction and maintenance.

The Foundation was able to secure Congressional sponsorship for legislation to authorize the Navy Memorial Foundation to construct a Navy Memorial on public land in the District of Columbia. Congress authorized the Memorial in 1980, with the stipulation that funding come solely from private contributions. Public Law 96-199, an omnibus bill for the Department of the Interior, was signed into law in March 1980 by President Jimmy Carter, a former Navy lieutenant.

Paralleling the legislative process, the Foundation dealt with the design of the memorial-to-be. How and where do you build a Navy Memorial on land? What is an adequate representation or symbol? Capital designer L'Enfant chose a column, a popular 18th-century form of architectural adulation, to be located on the banks of the Potomac River. But a column isn't too functional, and early on, the Foundation sought a memorial that would be functional as a "living memorial," specifically that would provide a concert stage to be used by all the military bands based in Washington.

The Foundation then "discovered" the Pennsylvania Avenue Development Corporation, and together, the two organizations brought their dreams together in the selection of Market Square as the site for the Navy Memorial, to help fulfill PADC's dream of bringing life back to Pennsylvania Avenue. In partnership with PADC, the Foundation participated in the selection of Conklin Rossant architects of New York.

The architects' first design was a massive arch, a Washington version of the Arc de Triomphe in Paris. All but one of the approving agencies thought the arch would be just wonderful, but the National Capital Planning Commission rejected the plan—a blow and a blessing to the struggling Foundation. However

Market Square neighbors Don W. Wilson, Archivist of the United States, and Rear Admiral Thompson at their new Metro Station pylon on Pennsylvania Avenue.

demoralizing a setback, Rear Admiral Thompson and his lieutenants returned to the drawing boards and came up with a concept for the design that was to become the Navy Memorial you see today.

Instead of a massive and costly arch that blocks an important vista across Pennsylvania Avenue, the Navy Memorial offers the low and subtle profile of a 100-foot diameter amphitheater and plaza, whose deck is a granite map of the world, surrounded by fountains and pools.

"To passers-by, the appearance of the Memorial is not unlike that of America's perceptions of the sea," says Admiral Thompson. "Even though it is vast and broad and unmistakably there, you could miss seeing it if you are not paying attention. But when you walk on to the site, it engulfs you with its scale and grandeur."

The total area of the Navy Memorial is 53,879 square feet, with a supporting foundation of 3,543 cubic yards of concrete and 150 tons of reinforcing steel. The Memorial is covered with 5,112 pieces of cut stone, mostly granite, weighing a total of 860 tons.

Meantime, the Foundation selected a sculptor, Stanley Bleifeld of Connecticut, and, it was later

Thousands of chairs block off Pennsylvania Avenue to await guests attending the dedication of the Navy Memorial on October 13, 1987.

Admiral and Mrs. Arleigh A. Burke at the launching of *USS Arleigh Burke (DDC-51)*, September 16, 1989.

learned, a Navy veteran who illustrated training manuals during World War II. Bleifeld refined the seascape plaza concept and introduced to it the first sketches of a solitary figure, a sailor, later dubbed by the Foundation the Lone Sailor. Additional sketches would follow, including those of a sailor and his family for The Homecoming statue located in the Visitors Center.

Geographic, architectural and artistic issues aside, the Foundation was all the while engaged in raising funds for the Memorial, through the creation of the Navy Memorial Log and a corporate giving program. By 1992, Log enrollments (representing minimum contributions of $25 per name) had exceeded 190,000 names. Log enrollments continue to be accepted today and will be accepted as long as the Memorial exists.

By December 1985, the Foundation had raised enough funds to warrant a go-ahead approval from the Secretary of the Interior, and construction got

underway that month. (The Foundation staff and Board of Directors had raised $15-million by

. . . . . . . . . . . . . . . . . .

*"Concerts on the Avenue"
have rapidly become
a permanent and popular
summertime tradition
on the Washington scene.*

. . . . . . . . . . . . . . . . . .

opening day of the Visitors Center, and fund raising continues today, to retire remaining construction debt and support educational programs undertaken by the Foundation.)

By August 1987, Stanley Bleifeld completed work on the Lone Sailor statue as construction of the Memorial neared completion.

October 13, 1987 was the long awaited official dedication of the U. S. Navy Memorial, the 212th

birthday of the United States Navy. The Navy brought out the big guns on the portico of the National Archives across the street from the Memorial: the Secretary of Defense, the Secretary of the Navy, the Chairman of the Joints Chiefs of Staff, the Chief of Naval Operations, the Master Chief Petty Officer of the Navy. Nearly all of their living predecessors gathered in the audience, including Admiral Arleigh A. Burke. In far larger numbers were Navy veterans from all over America.

The Memorial came to life that blustery October day, but not many visitors returned to the Memorial until the following summer of 1988, with the premiere of "Concerts on the Avenue," a weekly series of evening concerts by the U. S. Navy

The U.S. Navy Band performs at a summer evening "Concert on the Avenue."

14

Band and other service bands and their supporting units in the Washington area. "Concerts on the Avenue" have rapidly become a permanent and popular summertime tradition on the Washington scene.

From late 1987 to mid-1990, builders erected two commercial mixed-use buildings on the northern perimeter of the Memorial. The eastern-most of the two buildings was selected for the Memorial's 24-thousand square foot Visitors Center. The building's shell was sufficiently completed by September 1989 to permit contractors to begin fitting out the Visitors Center and the Foundation's offices. Occupying leased space on the ground floor and concourse level below it, the Visitors Center houses a magnificent motion picture theater, a Ship's Store, the U. S. Presidents Room and the Navy Memorial Log Room.

The U. S. Navy Memorial Log is a special tribute to the contributions and service of naval veterans—past, present and future. The Log is a computerized record of present and former Navy personnel who have contributed or on whose behalf funds have been given to the Memorial's building fund. Log

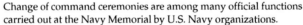

*The U.S. Navy Memorial Log is a special tribute to the contributions and service of naval veterans—past, present and future.*

entries include the name, highest rank or rate held, place and date of birth, and the dates of naval service of each person enrolled. The Log continuously scrolls on a large video screen. In addition, visitors to the Log Room may retrieve specific names on a screen to see ancestors, loved ones, friends or themselves immortalized with other Navy heroes listed in the Log. Enrollment

For the dedication of the U.S. Navy Memorial, October 13, 1987, Pennsylvania Avenue was closed off and paved with a blue carpet from 7th to 9th Streets. Four Navy bands participated in the event.

in the Log is also open to members of the Marine Corps and Coast Guard who have served with the U. S. Navy or whose units operated with the Navy and World War II Merchant Marine veterans.

At long last, the Visitors Center opened in June 1991 and was formally dedicated on October 12, 1991, during the Navy Birthday weekend. The Memorial and its Visitors Center will continue to evolve over the next few years, becoming, in the eyes of one founder, "the crown jewel of Pennsylvania Avenue." For now, the dream is fulfilled, if not paid for, as the key elements of a great and wonderful Memorial are drawn together—as surely connected as the separate dreams of an 18th-century architect, a President of the United States and a distinguished Navy admiral.

Change of command ceremonies are among many official functions carried out at the Navy Memorial by U.S. Navy organizations.

# The Map of the World

## Amphitheater for a Living Memorial, Visual Reminder of Expanse of the Sea

The 100-foot diameter granite map in the amphitheater floor of the Navy Memorial is the largest map of the world, but the map's most lasting distinction may be the way it was built rather than its size. Craftsmen achieved an unprecedented level of stone cutting accuracy in order to create an unusually detailed map in the difficult medium of granite.

Based on a computerized enlargement of an azimuthal projection purchased from the Defense Mapping Agency, the 1/10th-scale map centers on Washington, D.C., which serves as the point of North-South alignment. The map is constructed of a two-inch layer of granite weighing 27.71 pounds per square foot, with a total map area of 7,853.98 square feet and weight of 108.82 tons. Stonecutters

from New England Stone Industries, Inc., Smithfield, Rhode Island, used an advanced technology employing a thin stream of liquid under extremely high pressure to cut the map's land and sea areas. The cutting method represents a breakthrough in stone cutting which will have widespread and lasting impact on architecture, sculpture and construction techniques.

Computer controlled and robot operated, the highly sophisticated machines have been used in other industries to cut multiple layers of fabrics, aircraft engine parts, disposable diapers and a wide range of other materials, particularly where other cutting techniques would change the materials being cut. Manufacturers cut steel and other metals without

tempering the materials with heat; bakeries even use the liquid jet to cut cake, leaving behind neither crumbs nor soggy cake slices.

Liquid jet cutting methods did not reach the stone cutting field until the Navy Memorial design posed a challenge: create a very detailed map of the world in granite. Using conventional carbide cutting wheels or diamond band saws would have sacrificed considerable detail.

The liquid jet is a stream of water and grit slurry about 1/32nd of an inch, under 60-thousand pounds of pressure. The cut is very smooth, clean and quick, cutting up to two inches a minute on straight cuts, slowing down to one-half inch a minute for detailed curve cuts.

Two types of granite were used, Laurentide from Canada for ocean areas, and Deer Isle from Maine for land areas. The water and slurry cutting was used only for coastal outlines. Cutters used conventional methods to cut latitude and longitude lines which cross-hatch the ocean areas forming the largest expanse of the globe.

Every liquid jet cut was made twice, once on the 'ocean' granite and once on the 'land' granite, with

Rear Admiral Thompson, watches a computer- and robot-operated nozzle cut through 2-inch thick granite to create a section of the Memorial's "Granite Sea."

Construction proceeds on the northwest water cascade (top), the granite map (center) and the complete site—as seen shortly before the 1987 dedication.

would be a bump of 3/8th of a inch and barely noticed on surface of the map—a rough and tough fire-hardened finish for durability and good traction for pedestrians.

## Visual Aid for Students of Geography

The Navy Memorial Foundation planned all along for the granite map to give visitors a better grasp of the vastness of ocean areas compared to the land masses. But it did not readily occur to the Foundation that the map would attract school teachers and their classes to the Memorial for a quick lesson in geography! This has happened often enough to encourage the staff to appoint a professional educator to develop lesson plans for geography teachers. The plan is now available from the Navy Memorial Foundation.

All of this fits in nicely with the Memorial's long-planned objective of contributing to public understanding of the Navy and the environment of the sea.

## Fountains and Pools

Surrounding the map are four water pools, two along the northern perimeter each holding 8,737 gallons of water, and two on the southern perimeter each holding 22,599 gallons. The waters in all four pools have been authentically "spiked" with waters from the Seven Seas.

The pools have separate fountain systems that together pump 249,000 gallons per hour or 950 gallons per minute for each of the smaller pools and 1,125 gallons per minute for each of the larger pools.

Pool and fountain pumps are located below ground along the northeastern quadrant of the Memorial. Adjacent to the underground pump rooms are dressing rooms for performers and storage for portable seating for the Memorial's summertime "Concerts on the Avenue."

the adjoining pieces glued together for an extremely tight fit.

On the map's scale, one inch equals less than 12 miles on the earth. A walk across the grid map might give one the feel for one of the Navy's newest frontiers, outer space. A person whose eye level is between five and six feet off the grid map is at a scale height of 700 to 800 miles above the earth depicted on the grid.

Designers wondered whether scaling of the map should incorporate some bumps on the land surfaces to represent mountain ranges. They discarded the idea after figuring that Mount Everest

## Eight Nations
## Contributed to Memorial

*"TO SHIPMATES FROM OTHER LANDS—THE WATERS THAT DIVIDE US, UNITE US."*

These are the words inscribed on the exterior granite wall of the International Pool, the fountain pool located on the southwestern quarter of the Memorial.

The navies or governments of eight nations have contributed funds to help the Navy Memorial. Through the auspices of their own navies, eight nations thus far have made generous contributions to our building fund, and the Navy Memorial Foundation is extremely grateful for their support. Gifts ranging from $65-thousand to $150-thousand have been received from the Argentine Republic, Australia, Republic of China, Republic of France, Federal Republic of Germany, Japan, Republic of Korea and Spain. These country names were the first to be inscribed on the pool wall; starting from the center, the names are being added left and right in the order in which the countries make their contributions.

Architects at the National Guard Armory in Providence, Rhode Island, inspect the plastic sheeting which forms the template for cutting the Memorial's granite map.

Admiral Arleigh A. Burke (top) and his wife (standing at Washington, D.C.) explore the Memorial's granite map of the world. Lone Sailor statue is at right.

# The Lone Sailor

The Lone Sailor statue represents all people who ever served, are serving now or who are yet to serve in the Navy. The Lone Sailor is a composite of the U. S. Navy bluejacket, past, present and future. He's called the Lone Sailor, yet he is hardly ever alone, standing there on the broad granite plaza which forms the amphitheater of the Navy Memorial. Visitors to the Memorial are immediately drawn to him—to peer into his farseeing eyes, to admire him or size him up, to see if he's as tough or as gentle as he seems. Visitors find that he is all that he seems and probably more.

The founders of the Navy Memorial envisioned this Lone Sailor as 25 years old at most, a senior second class petty officer who is fast becoming a seagoing veteran. He has done it all—fired his weapons in a dozen wars, weighed anchor from a thousand ports, tracked supplies, doused fires, repelled boarders, typed in quadruplicate and mess-cooked, too. He has made liberty call in great cities and tiny villages, where he played tourist, ambassador, missionary to the poor, adventurer, souvenir shopper and friend to new lands. His shipmates remember him with pride and tell their grandchildren stories, some of which, like him, are seven feet tall.

The bronze statue is the creation of Stanley Bleifeld, U. S. Navy Memorial's official sculptor, selected by a board of recognized art authorities from a field of 36 sculptors identified in a six month, nationwide search. A native of New York City, Bleifeld maintains a studio at his home in Weston, Connecticut, and also in Pietrasanta, Italy.

By coincidence, Bleifeld served in the Navy in World War II. Like many other talented artists at the time, he was assigned as an illustrator for Navy training manuals; he never went into battle, but he helped train those who did.

After so long an absence from the Navy, Bleifeld visited the fleet and other Navy activities to help him see anew the American sailor in the sea environment; he further focused his impressions in meetings with the Secretary of the Navy, the Chief of Naval Operations and other senior officer and enlisted personnel.

Then began the evolution of the Lone Sailor, at first a general image in the eyes of the sculptor and his patrons—the Navy Memorial Foundation officers, staff

Rear Admiral Thompson and sculptor Stanley Bleifeld flank the Lone Sailor aboard the delivery van on the statue's arrival at the Memorial.

and board members. These patrons represented literally hundreds of years of Navy experience and acquaintance with the Lone Sailor.

"In an evolving process we considered five different images—an oil painting and four miniature clay statues—as to which could best impart the message we wished to convey," said Rear Admiral William Thompson, president of the Navy Memorial Foundation. "The only surviving piece of proposed statuary from the original concept is

"The Liberty Hound," an early concept of a lone sailor statue, now stands in the Navy Memorial in Jacksonville, Florida.

the Lone Sailor; he was conceived to be almost exactly the way he now appears."

But there were some intervening variations, as if the whole conceptual process deliberately led off course in order to come back and safely reach port.

Bleifeld's first model was a sailor in dress blues with a pea coat slung over his shoulder. Close, but that was not "him."

"We thought he should be wearing the pea coat," says Thompson, "still one of the best government issues known to man and a piece of clothing that is universally recognized."

The first model needed a few more years of service, some maturity added to his face, making him a veteran of the seas; it was nicknamed "the Boot." "Put some wind in his canvas," Bleifeld was told.

Bleifeld's response was magnificent, an excellent piece of sculpture which received

· · · · · · · · · · · · · · · · · · · ·

*The Lone Sailor is impressive. "You would want this guy at your battle station when it's not a drill."*

· · · · · · · · · · · · · · · · · · · ·

immediate applause. It was of a handsome young man with mischievous look toward the sea while he leaned forward with one foot on a cleat. He was a cocky, confident, good looking sailor whom the office staff dubbed "Liberty Hound," because he looked like he was eagerly awaiting the first boat ashore.

"We all loved this strong and brash young man of the sea, but because he was leaning over the cleat, he did not give us the scale or elevation we wanted in an upright presentation," says Admiral

Thompson. "As it turns out, he was exactly the right image for a Navy memorial being developed on the riverfront in Jacksonville, Florida. We were pleased to make him available to Jacksonville and are extremely grateful to the citizens of Jacksonville for their support to the Navy Memorial in Washington."

The next model was of a sailor huddled in a pea coat with collar turned up, hiding most of his face. Closer yet, but still not "him."

"We wanted to see him as a young sailor with good physical stature—strong and resolute. We asked Stanley to open up the pea coat at the neck to show more of a strong face and more of the dress blues and neckerchief. And we asked for a dynamic appearance of standing before a brisk wind," says Thompson.

Meantime, Thompson and his staff had developed a guidance paper which Bleifeld skillfully transformed into a final eloquent working model and vision of the Lone Sailor as he appears today at the Navy Memorial. This new version could truly represent American Bluejackets in all of their manifestations since 1775.

The Foundation's board of directors approved the fourth model and directed Admiral Thompson to obtain required approvals from the Pennsylvania Avenue Development Corporation, the U. S. Commission of Fine Arts, the National Capital Planning Commission and the Secretary of the Interior.

Bleifeld's initial rendering of this fourth Lone Sailor was 22-inches tall, about one fourth the size of the finished statue. When the aforementioned Washington agencies approved the maquette, Bleifeld proceeded to "scale up" to a full sized clay model at his Connecticut studio. He built a steel framework complete with interior water piping to support and provide moisture for his clay medium. He completed the clay mold in the spring of 1987.

When the life-size version was approved, Bleifeld drenched the model with a plaster coating to make a negative mold, and—the last step in his Connecticut studios—created a plaster positive to ship to the Tallix Foundry in Beacon, New York.

The Tallix Foundry, which specializes in service to the art community, is owned by Richard Polich, who was a commissioned naval officer in the late 1950s. Mr. Polich completed the jet aircraft training syllabus in November 1957 and flew the Navy's F-9 jet fighters until he left active duty in 1959 as a lieutenant junior grade.

Tallix used Bleifeld's positive to pour sectional rubber negatives, and these were used to make positive wax molds 3/16ths of an inch thick, the thickness of the statue's hollow bronze shell. Tallix craftsmen carefully cleaned the wax positives and attached to them an elaborate system of wax runners or gates. Then they surrounded the wax tubes and shells, inside and out, with a strong ceramic shell.

As each ceramic shell was autoclaved to a temperature of 1800-degrees Fahrenheit, the wax positive was lost—melted out of the remaining mold—leaving space for the final pouring of bronze, which occurred on August 4, 1987.

At the request of Admiral Thompson, Polich had his workers melt into the bronze for the Lone Sailor artifacts from eight U. S. Navy ships, provided by Henry A. Vadnais, Jr., curator for the Navy at the Naval Historical Center in the Washington Navy Yard. The ships span the Navy's history, yielding small pieces of copper sheeting, spikes, hammock hooks and other fragments from the post-revolutionary frigates *Constitution* ("Old Ironsides") and *Constellation*; the steamer *Hartford*, flagship of Admiral David G. Farragut in the Civil War era; the battleship *USS Maine*; the iron-hulled steamer/sailing ship *USS Ranger*; the World War II-era cruiser *USS Biloxi* and aircraft carrier *USS Hancock*, and the nuclear-powered submarine *USS Seawolf*. One last addition was a personal decoration from today's Navy, one given to sailors in war and peace, the National Defense Service Medal. These bits of metal are now part of the Lone Sailor.

After the bronze sections were poured, cooled and sandblasted, the foundry welded them together for the very last step, patination—a heat and chemical treatment to achieve controlled oxidation yielding the distinctive color of the statue as it appears today.

Stanley Bleifeld (wearing glasses) works on the final clay rendering of the Lone Sailor statue.

Bleifeld worked on the Lone Sailor creation for more than a year, and the technical processes took several additional months, with all of the effort focused on unveiling at the formal dedication of the Memorial on October 13, 1987. On that day, Bleifeld went home to begin work on his next sculpture for the Memorial, "The Homecoming."

Reaction to the Lone Sailor has been gratifying. "He certainly represents us," is the claim heard

. . . . . . . . . . . . . . . . . . . .

*"He is the classic American sailor. That statue looks like bronze, but there is plenty of salt, paint, sweat, fuel oil and courage stirred in."*

. . . . . . . . . . . . . . . . . . . .

from nearly every Navy community, active or retired. The Navy Memorial Foundation regularly receives telephone calls or notes from Navy veterans or their families wondering where the Foundation obtained their photograph as the model for the statue. The Lone Sailor is impressive to people who have never served in the Navy and powerfully so for those who have served.

"You would want this guy at your battle station when it's not a drill," former Master Chief Petty Officer of the Navy Billy C. Sanders says of The Lone Sailor. "He is the classic American sailor. That statue looks like bronze, but there is plenty of salt, paint, sweat, fuel oil and courage stirred in."

The Lone Sailor here exhibits more patience and courage than the real-life people he represents!

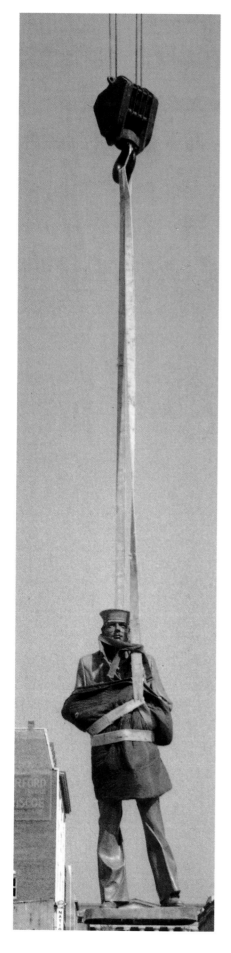

Skyscraper crane lowers the Lone Sailor to his permanent duty station at the Navy Memorial.

26

## The Lone Sailor

## The Final Guidance

Following is the text of the final guidance for the creation of the Lone Sailor statue. It was drafted by Rear Admiral William Thompson, president of the Navy Memorial Foundation, and Captain Walter "R" Thomas, USN (Ret.), a member of Thompson's staff.

*The "Lone Sailor" is the singular symbolic figure of the U. S. Navy Memorial complex. He is a composite of the U. S. Navy Bluejacket—relatively young, about 26—and a senior second class petty officer who is fast maturing to become a sea-going veteran. He is the kid from down the street who left to join the Navy just a few years ago. Since then, he has been to Navy schools and off to sea, shipping out in different types of ships that have crossed the equator, the Arctic Circle and the international dateline. Sea duty continues to have the aura of romance—the adventure of more ports to visit, more miles to log, more training, more duties, more experience and more responsibilities—now performed with the seasoning of a veteran sailor who has been there before and is willing to go back.*

*He embodies two hundred years of world-wide experience, loyalty and courage, and he is a member of the world's best navy. The seas enchant him; he is fascinated by each ocean's beauty and peacefulness, as well as its emotions and its strengths, manifested when the seas roil to awesome exhibitions of typhoon fury and savagery. His personal demeanor exudes confidence, and he has a subtle swagger in his walk. He believes firmly in himself, his ship, his leaders and his Navy.*

*The "Lone Sailor" is pensive but alert as he surveys the sea. As he gazes out on the ocean that surrounds him, he ponders that wide domain where his country has asked him to serve—that vast area that covers more than three quarters of the earth's surface and which has historically claimed many of his shipmates who have fallen to its perils. The comfort and beauty of the seas usually warm him, but his serenity is often punctured by his knowledge of the powerful turbulence of the seas in turmoil. Still, he retains a special quality of love and respect for the sea.*

*In the distance, far beyond the horizon, is the United States— home! At sea, home is always over the horizon, in all its meanings— his roots, his loved ones, his natural habitat, his patriotism—all more real to him than described in even the best lyrics of sea songs and chanteys.*

*"Home and the sea" hold the answers to all questions for the professional U. S. Navy Bluejacket.*

# Inscriptions in Granite, Lessons in Blood

THE UNITED STATES NAVY MEMORIAL

IN HONOR OF THOSE WHO SERVED TO FORGE THE
HERITAGE OF THE UNITED STATES NAVY

IN TRIBUTE TO THOSE WHO PERISHED TO PROVIDE PEACE
AND SECURITY FOR OUR MARITIME NATION

IN GRATITUDE TO THOSE NOW SERVING

T hese words inscribed in the marble paving above the compass rose at the entrance to the Memorial define the meaning and purpose of the Memorial. The compass rose, a large bronze casting encircled by bronze rings and white granite, is bracketed by two flag masts, forming both a main entrance to the Memorial from Pennsylvania Avenue and a ceremonial area for the Memorial. The compass rose recalls one of the earliest and still-used navigational instruments, with the cardinal and intercardinal points surrounding the Navy seal; the compass is aligned to Magnetic North, a few degrees off the Memorial's alignment to true North.

A few steps farther into the Memorial plaza and perimeter are defined the traditions of America's bond with the sea. The plaza is encircled by a granite ring of walls and steps on which are inscribed important lessons and memorable quotes from naval history.

At the main entrance to the Memorial, imbedded in the granite paving north of the compass rose . . .

ANY MAN WHO MAY BE ASKED IN THIS CENTURY
WHAT HE DID TO MAKE HIS LIFE WORTHWHILE . . .
CAN RESPOND WITH A GOOD DEAL OF PRIDE AND SATISFACTION,
"I SERVED IN THE UNITED STATES NAVY."

*President John F. Kennedy, August 1, 1963*
*United States Naval Academy, Annapolis, Maryland*

Addressing a new class of midshipmen entering the Naval Academy, President Kennedy drew from his own experience as a naval officer in World War II. Commissioned an Ensign in October 1941, Kennedy undertook torpedo boat training in 1942 and later took command of PT-109 in the Pacific. He was awarded the Navy and Marine Corps Medal for heroism following the collision and sinking of his vessel by a Japanese destroyer in the Solomons. Kennedy directed the rescue of his crew, swimming many hours to secure aid and food after he got his crew ashore.

Aircraft Carrier

# WHOSOEVER CAN HOLD THE SEA HAS COMMAND OF EVERYTHING.

*Themistocles (524-460 B.C.)*

Themistocles was an Athenian statesman and, as his admonition suggests, a strong proponent of naval expansion. These remarks are attributed to him in regard to the threat to Athens from invaders from Persia. Here is the classic and certainly one of the earliest lessons of sea power, a lesson which remains valid today as the U. S. Navy expresses its mission with terms like *sea control* and *power projection.*

. . . . . . . . . . . . . . . . . . . . . . . . . . . . . . . . . . . . . . . . . .

# I HAVE NOT YET BEGUN TO FIGHT!

*Captain John Paul Jones, September 23, 1779*

Fighting for survival on the sea as well as land during the American Revolution, the American Navy was pitted against the usually invincible Royal Navy. Borrowed from the French, Captain Jones' *Bonhomme Richard* was an old, converted merchant ship which tangled with the faster and more heavily armed *Serapis*. After several broadsides at close range, *Bonhomme Richard* had her hold flooded, guns out of commission, half her crew dead or wounded, rudder and rigging shot away. The British captain, Richard Pearson, called to Jones asking whether he had struck his colors. Jones roared back with his immortal words, thus inspiring his men with his own will to win. Realizing his only chance against *Serapis* was to close alongside, Jones engaged the enemy in a furious battle which reduced both ships to shambles. After four hours, the British captain himself hauled down the colors on his ship, which Jones then took over before *Bonhomme Richard* sank two days later. Of Jones' many contributions to the Navy's great traditions, none stands out more conspicuously than his refusal to acknowledge defeat—a philosophy since revered by embattled sailors throughout the history of the Navy.

. . . . . . . . . . . . . . . . . . . . . . . . . . . . . . . . . . . . . . . . . .

# SIGHTED SUB. SANK SAME.

*Aviation Machinist Mate 1st Class Donald F. Mason, January 28, 1942*

Petty Officer Mason was a Navy enlisted pilot flying a Lockheed Hudson PBO-1 out of Argentia, Newfoundland. In January, 1942, German U-Boats were sinking better than a ship a day. So America yearned for the first sinking of an enemy sub in American waters—as inferred in the terse but immensely inspiring message Mason sent after he dropped two depth charges on a U-Boat he spotted in the Atlantic. The irony of this episode is that the Mason's sub sinking was not confirmed and thus was not "a first;" however, 46 days later the newly promoted Chief Petty Officer Mason did sink the U-503, his first sinking and the second sub sunk in American waters. Facts and their order in history notwithstanding, Mason's message helped galvanize American public resolve and left for all time an apt and unadorned characterization of the dedicated, can-do American sailor.

Battleship

# ONE SMALL STEP FOR MAN, ONE GIANT LEAP FOR MANKIND.

*Neil A. Armstrong, July 20, 1969*

Astronaut and former naval aviator Neil Armstrong became the first man to set foot on the moon. The moon landing was then the culmination of a manned space flight program that began in 1961 with another Navy man, Commander Alan B. Shepard, Jr., becoming the first American in space with a sub-orbital flight from Cape Canaveral, Florida. The U. S. Navy has played an important role in America's space program since its inception, and America's astronaut program continues to draw on naval aviators like Armstrong and Shepard from the Navy and John Glenn from the Marine Corps. Now a Rear Admiral (retired), Alan Shepard is a member of the Navy Memorial Foundation's board of directors.

. . . . . . . . . . . . . . . . . . . . . . . . . . . . . . . . . . . . . . . . . . . . . . . .

# UNDERWAY ON NUCLEAR POWER.

*Commander Dennis Wilkinson, Commanding Officer, USS Nautilus (SSN-571), January 17, 1955*

The terse message signaled a new "transition of power" for the Navy, a Navy which was born under sail, reached adolescence in coal and matured in liquid fossil fuels. A decade after the birth of the atomic bomb, atomic energy was at last employed as a controlled and sustained source of power, fulfilling for the Navy the long held dream of a true submarine—able to operate beneath the surface almost indefinitely and thereby reducing detection to a minimum. Four years after *Nautilus* made her sea trials, Congress awarded a gold medal to its developer, Captain Hyman G. Rickover, for his achievements in developing nuclear power. Today, all submarines, most aircraft carriers and many surface combatants in the U. S. Navy are nuclear powered.

. . . . . . . . . . . . . . . . . . . . . . . . . . . . . . . . . . . . . . . . . . . . . . . .

# THE SEA IS AN UNNATURAL ENVIRONMENT FOR MAN, AND IT TAKES SOMETHING EXTRA FOR MEN TO LIVE WITH IT.

*Secretary of the Navy Paul H. Nitze, October 27, 1965*

What men (and now women) are these who give up the safety of good earth beneath their feet to venture into hostile nautical realms? From pre-historic times to the present, seafaring people have captured the awe and imagination of their shorebound friends. The attractions are obvious—commerce, discovery, food, recreation and, often, great wealth. But relatively few answer the call, for the challenge is daunting and the risk is great in almost every instance of man's encounter with the sea. Merchant seaman, fishermen, naval service personnel, oceanographers, engineers, oil workers—some would even add recreational sailors—are among this different breed of which Paul Nitze spoke. His October speech in Long Beach, California, occurred on what was then celebrated as Navy Day. Nitze served as the Navy's 58th Secretary of the Navy, from November 1963 to June 1967.

Amphibious Assault Ship

Destroyer Tender

# ... WITHOUT A DECISIVE NAVAL FORCE, WE CAN DO NOTHING DEFINITIVE. AND WITH IT, EVERYTHING HONOURABLE AND GLORIOUS.

*General George Washington, November 15, 1781*

Although the British commander Cornwallis had surrendered at Yorktown the month before, the final outcome of the War of the Revolution was not yet clear, and some naval combat would occur as late as 1783. In this uncertain climate, General Washington wrote to his friend and advisor, the young Marquis de LaFayette, "It follows then as certain as that night succeeds the day, that without a decisive naval force, we can do nothing definitive. And with it, everything honourable and glorious. A constant naval superiority would terminate the war speedily; without it, I do not know that it will ever be terminated honourably." Ironically, the American Navy ended that year with only two vessels in commission.

· · · · · · · · · · · · · · · · · · · · · · · · · · · · · · · · · · · · · · · · · · · · · · · · ·

# DON'T GIVE UP THE SHIP!

*Captain James Lawrence, June 1, 1813*

The new skipper and his ship *USS Chesapeake* were clearly no match for the British frigate *HMS Shannon* during their encounter in the War of 1812. Mortally wounded at the outset of the brief fight which ended in the capture of his ship, Lawrence was carried below uttering to his crew a battle cry that would inspire and save generations of sailors in battle but not his own command. Three months later in the battle of Lake Erie, Commodore Oliver Hazard Perry used the words of Lawrence on one of his battle flags.

· · · · · · · · · · · · · · · · · · · · · · · · · · · · · · · · · · · · · · · · · · · · · · · · ·

# WE HAVE MET THE ENEMY AND THEY ARE OURS.

*Commodore Oliver Hazard Perry, September 10, 1813*

In a dispatch to General William Henry Harrison, Perry thus summed up his triumph in the Battle of Lake Erie. The enemy in this case was two ships, two brigs, one schooner and one sloop, all British units engaging the new United States of America in the War of 1812. As a result of Perry's victory, the whole British position on and around Lake Erie collapsed like a house of cards. In less than a month, Perry was able to shift his warring ashore; on October 5, he personally lead a cavalry charge in the land battle of Thames for the American army under Harrison's command.

Dock Landing Ship

Guided Missile Cruiser

Fleet Oiler

Amphibious Transport Dock

# . . . UNCOMMON VALOR WAS A COMMON VIRTUE.

*Fleet Admiral Chester W. Nimitz, March 17, 1945*

The tiny island of Iwo Jima, at eight square miles—less than one-eighth the size of the District of Columbia—is 700 miles south of Tokyo. Although the island was heavily fortified with 21,000 Japanese troops, the American forces might have passed it by on their way to the conquest of Japan. But it was too important as an "unsinkable aircraft carrier" base for B-29 Superfortress bombers completing their bombing runs over Japan from mainland China to the west and the Marianas Islands to the south. Moreover, Iwo Jima would be an essential launch point for an eventual invasion of the Japanese home islands. The battle of Iwo Jima goes down in history as one of the most costly and frightful battles ever waged. The Japanese,

hidden in Iwo's caves and camouflaged block houses and with plenty of ammunition, were by now well familiar with the American's attack strategy. Landing from 800 invasion ships lying off the island, U. S. Marines dug in and inched forward while the Japanese kept up a murderous fire along the beaches below Mount Suribachi. After days of grueling battle, the Americans prevailed, but at a terrible cost to the Marines: 5,017 dead and 17,145 wounded. Nimitz, Commander of the Pacific Fleet, declared in his Pacific Fleet Communique No. 300, "The battle of Iwo Jima has been won. Among the Americans who served on Iwo, uncommon valor was a common virtue."

. . . . . . . . . . . . . . . . . . . . . . . . . . . . . . . . . . . . . . . . . . . . . .

# DAMN THE TORPEDOES—FULL SPEED AHEAD!

*Admiral David G. Farragut, August 5, 1864*

The naval leader who became the Navy's first Admiral entered the Navy before he was *nine years old*. By the time he came of age he was already experienced at shiphandling and leadership. When the Civil War broke out in 1861, Farragut had already served 49 years in the Navy. In the Battle of Mobile Bay, Farragut commanded his squadron from his flagship *Hartford*. During a critical phase of the battle against Confederate naval forces, Farragut's ships faced a Confederate mine field—mines were then called torpedoes. Undaunted and having armored his ships against just such a threat, Farragut uttered his stirring battle cry and pressed on to victory.

The strategic significance of this victory is either not realized or not fully appreciated by all but serious students of the Civil War. The Battle of Mobile Bay effectively closed off the Confederacy's last major port on the Gulf Coast—crippling the logistic pipeline to battlegrounds to the north. Farragut placed on the record of history a glowing example of the employment of naval forces against an enemy economically dependent on shipping. Denied the influx of supplies and reinforcement from overseas markets, the South was eventually starved for war material thanks in no small measure to Farragut's brilliance in strategic planning and daring in battle at sea.

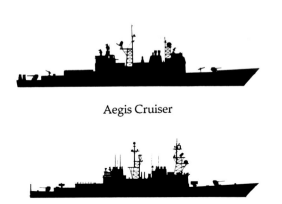

Aegis Cruiser

Guided Missile Destroyer

Destroyer

Ballistic Missile Submarine

# I WISH TO HAVE NO CONNECTION WITH ANY SHIP THAT DOES NOT SAIL FAST, FOR I INTEND TO GO IN HARM'S WAY. . .

*Captain John Paul Jones, November 1778*

Extending his string of Revolutionary War victories with his capture of the British sloop-of-war *Drake* on the coast of Ireland in April 1778, Captain John Paul Jones sailed to France. There he began his quest for a ship that would enable him to exact a further toll on the British in their own waters. He was offered an old East Indiaman, *Le Duc de Duras*, but Jones wanted something better. After exchanges of correspondence with Benjamin Franklin and friends in France and American agents abroad, Jones considered offers of several captured British ships. He rejected these outright: "I wish to have no connection with any ship that does not sail fast, for I intend to go in in harm's way...I would rather be shott (sic) ashore than sent to Sea in such things as the Armed Prizes I have described." By December 1778, Jones settled for the original offer of *Le Duc de Duras*, which he renamed *Bonhomme Richard*, and on whose decks a year later he would say "I have not yet begun to fight."

. . . . . . . . . . . . . . . . . . . . . . . . . . . . . . . . . . . .

On the north steps of the Memorial appear these familiar words:

ETERNAL FATHER, STRONG TO SAVE,
WHOSE ARM DOTH BIND THE RESTLESS WAVE,
WHO BIDD'ST THE MIGHTY OCEAN DEEP,
ITS OWN APPOINTED LIMITS KEEP;
O HEAR US WHEN WE CRY TO THEE
FOR THOSE IN PERIL ON THE SEA.

"Eternal Father" was written by William Whiting in 1860 and set to music by John B. Dykes in 1861. The Navy began using this hymn in divine services in 1879, and over the years it has come to be known as "The Navy Hymn."

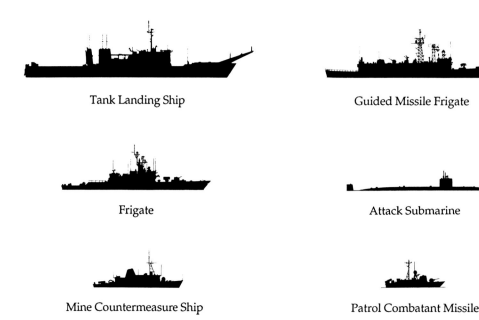

Tank Landing Ship

Guided Missile Frigate

Frigate

Attack Submarine

Mine Countermeasure Ship

Patrol Combatant Missile

# The Bronze Reliefs

The southern hemisphere of the Navy Memorial's 100-foot diameter granite map of the world is framed by 22 bronze reliefs. Set in deep relief, these lustrous 36x32-inch panels commemorate events in naval history or honor communities of the naval service—past and present.

Mounted on twin granite sculpture walls facing Pennsylvania Avenue, the bronze reliefs eloquently affirm the heritage and educational focus of the Memorial.

Art authorities have told the Navy Memorial Foundation that this may be the largest bronze relief program ever attempted in American art.

The Navy Memorial appointed a multi-talented artist, art historian and educator, Leo C. Irrera, of Washington, D.C., to undertake the massive challenge of overall design concept, creative development, and coordination with sculptors, foundries and local agencies with approval authority. Mr. Irrera personally sculpted three of the

bronze reliefs. A former executive assistant for the Foundation, Captain Robert S. Jones, USN (Ret.), served as the Bronze Relief Program Manager, principally managing fund raising programs and liaison between the Foundation and government agencies. Together with their team of ten sculptors and the generous support of all the sponsoring communities and organizations, Mr. Irrera and Captain Jones completed the development and installation of all

J. Carter Brown, Chairman, The Commission of Fine Arts, inspects the Sculpture Wall with Sculpture Coordinator Leo Irrera and Bronze Relief Project Officer Captain Robert S. Jones.

22 bronze reliefs in time to coincide with the summer 1991 opening of the Visitors Center.

The Foundation started out with some 60 subjects, and it could have been more. Requests for proposed subjects had gone to the Naval War College, the Naval Academy, the Naval Curator Emeritus of the Smithsonian, the Director of Naval History and the Naval Historical Foundation, as well as to members of the Foundation Board of Directors.

Of the more than 60 subjects which were suggested, some were parochial, some historical. With only 22 granite stones available on the sculpture walls, many decisions had to be made before the list was pared down to the final subjects. And, even as the first reliefs were being sculpted, final decisions on the last bronzes still remained to be made.

Originally, it was thought that the reliefs would be placed in a chronological order, so that as viewers progressed they would follow the history of the Navy. As Sculptor Coordinator, Leo Irrera, points out in his essay which

* * * * * * * * * * * * * * * *

*The Navy Memorial is a tribute to people. There are no guns, shells or other military hardware placed on the Memorial.*

* * * * * * * * * * * * * * * *

follows, the chronological sequence was scrapped.

In choosing the subjects, attention was paid to having as many eras of naval history depicted as possible. While a high percentage of the Navy veterans who visit the Memorial participated in World War II, the Foundation did not want to emphasize that particular conflict. Rather, it wanted to cover the broad expanse of the history, not only of the Navy, but also of the nation.

The Navy Memorial is a tribute to people. There are no guns, shells or other military hardware placed on the Memorial. Top priority for the subjects of the sculptures, therefore, went to presenting non-

military accomplishments of the Navy such as exploration and research. Few of the reliefs show combat operations.

Requirements dictated that a single scene be depicted in the sculpture—no montages were to be approved. So the last hurdle, from a subject perspective, came from choosing "the scene" after the basic subject had been selected, and then ensuring that the depiction was technically and historically accurate.

## Sponsorship of Bronze Reliefs

Each of the panels represents a sponsored investment goal of $50,000, which covers the cost of the bronze relief and the overall relief program.

The Navy Memorial Foundation is extremely grateful for the outstanding support given to the bronze reliefs by their sponsoring communities, who are identified in the following pages with pictures and information about their respective bronze reliefs. The visions and stories imparted by the bronze reliefs will be an enduring lesson on America's proud naval heritage for generations to come.

* * * * * * * * * * * * * * * * * * * * * * * * * * * * * * * * * * * * * * * * * * *

## Locator Legend

The number listed with a bronze relief title and appearing on a Sculpture Wall drawing at the bottom of these pages refers to the page where a photo of the work appears.

## West Sculpture Wall

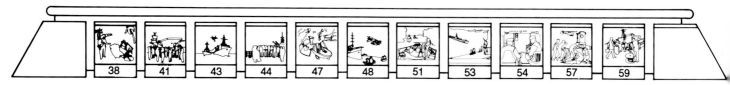

# Bronze Relief Sculptures: Concept, Process, Fulfillment

Leo C. Irrera, *Sculptor Coordinator*

From the start, it was decided that the sculpture walls of the Navy Memorial would manifest the Navy through depictions of historic naval events and recognition of its various components. This was one consideration; another consideration was the audience—its make-up and its interests.

The unique location of the memorial guarantees an audience of considerable size—local residents and tourists. Some would know a great deal about the U. S. Navy; most would know very little. Some would be sticklers for details; others would just want a good show— perhaps especially children (for whose benefit the sculptures are set on their granite walls close to the ground). There was, however, no guarantee that if indeed the audience looked, it would keep looking. So the overriding objective in the creation of the 22 bronze reliefs was to present a show that would hold the viewer without sacrificing the initial concept.

The president and board of directors of the Navy Memorial Foundation chose the components to be represented—the objective being to represent the Navy as more than "warships at sea." Because of the limitation of 22 spaces, many important naval components and events had to be omitted, so the most difficult task up front was the selection of 22 scenes that would best present a comprehensive picture of U. S. Navy people.

Captain Robert S. Jones, USN (Ret.) the Navy Memorial's bronze relief project manager, and I, as sculptor coordinator, met with the sponsors of the individual bronze reliefs to determine the subject matter for each plaque. The question posed to each was, "What is the desired viewer reaction? What would you like the viewer to come away with?" The general response was, "We'd like the viewer to learn something about us and to want to learn more."

The sculptors were selected not only for their talent and experience—all had a record of achievement—but also for their ability to respond to a client's needs and perhaps more importantly to involve the viewer. It was also essential that they could hold up to the many changes that would be necessitated by the sponsors and the various reviewing agencies as well as meeting the objectives, which were now refined to show:

- The U.S. Navy is indeed more than warships at sea.
- It takes a variety of skills and specialties to run our Navy.
- It also takes a good deal of support to keep it running, not the least of which is the Navy family.

To enhance viewers' involvement with the reliefs, certain creative devices were employed. It will be noticed on the sculpture walls that chronological arrangement has been avoided, that there are some closeups, some long shots and a variety of points of view. Additionally, characters in some of the reliefs are looking out from the scene to make eye contact and to engage the viewer. The differences in creative styles and techniques of the various sculptors adds a sense of discovery and excitement to the walk along the sculpture wall.

Taken individually and together, all 22 of the bronze reliefs accomplish their important purposes—to attract their audience, to promote understanding and appreciation of the art and the message, and to honor the people of the naval services.

## East Sculpture Wall

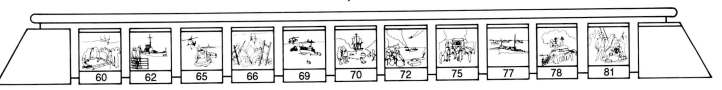

NAVAL CONSTRUCTION BATTALIONS
"Seabees Can Do"
SCULPTOR: LEO C. IRRERA

# Naval Construction Battalions

## "Seabees Can Do"

Leo C. Irrera, *Sculptor*

**C**onstrutmus Batuimus—"We build, we fight." Authorized on January 5, 1942, and officially established and named on March 5, 1942, the Navy's construction battalions—the world-renowned Seabees—have distinguished themselves in a half century of service in construction and combat. Early on they gained public recognition by building airstrips in the South Pacific while combat raged around them, the scene depicted in Leo Irrera's bronze relief. The sculpture was dedicated at the Navy Memorial on January 5, 1992, as one of the first events in the celebration of the Seabees Fiftieth Anniversary.

The Seabees first action came on Guadalcanal in August 1942, where they used abandoned Japanese equipment. In five days they had the airstrip ready for Marine fighter aircraft.

Seabees were part of every Pacific amphibious operation. From Guadalcanal, on up the islands of the western Pacific, the Seabees constructed bases and more airstrips. Landing with the initial invasion waves, the Seabees attached floating pontoons to amphibious craft such as LSTs to expedite the off-loading of equipment. Using their bulldozers, they often cleared a jungle path for advancing troops.

During World War II, the Seabees numbered about 240,000 men, formed into some 140 battalions. Their accomplishments include the construction of more than 400 advance bases—some accommodating 50,000 men—and housing facilities for 1.5-million personnel. In addition to air bases, they built shipyards, port and harbor works, training facilities, ammunition plants, fuel depots, floating and graving docks of all sizes. They accomplished these herculean tasks often under hostile fire.

The Seabees played a critical role in Korea and later in the Vietnam conflict which saw 26,000 Seabees serving. In the early 1990s the Seabees continued to distinguish themselves during Desert Storm in the Persian Gulf.

Today, Seabees play an important role in the U.S. Navy as its builders, engineers and humanitarians under their motto, "Seabees Can Do!" And, "What is difficult is done at once, what is impossible takes a little bit longer."

Seabees serve under the leadership of the commissioned officers of the Civil Engineer Corps, who are the engineers and architects who manage the Navy's shore facilities and who oversee the construction and maintenance of the shore establishment. In addition, they command the field forces that construct advance bases for support of Marine and Navy operations around the world.

The Seabees bronze relief is sponsored by past and present Seabees, officers of the Navy Civil Engineering Corps, and organizations such as the Seabee Memorial Scholarship Foundation. The sculptor for the relief, Leo C. Irrera, served as a Seabee in the Pacific during World War II.

Seabees lay steel mats during the construction of new bomber airfield on Bougainville, December 1943.

# The Navy Family

## "They who wait also serve"

Robert Lamb, *Sculptor*

**S**ailors are, after all, people. Like their land-locked cousins, they walk, talk, drive, eat, sleep, work, play, and in time, find a mate, get married, settle down and raise a family. Well, *maybe* settle down; that's the one thing that distinguishes a Navy family from almost all others. There is nothing very settled down about the separation imposed by long deployments at sea. History has seen Navy families—wives, children, and mothers and fathers, sisters, brothers and lately, even husbands standing on piers as their sailors departed for long deployments overseas.

During their sailors' absence, it is the families who have had the responsibility of keeping the home fires burning—seeing to the children's health and education, paying the bills, keeping the car running, and cutting the grass.

After each period of separation comes a happy ending as the sailors return from the sea. The sailors "man the rails" and keep eyes focused in search for that special family member waiting on the dock. And on the pier, families wait, dressed in their Sunday best, while banners are strung and the Navy band strikes up a welcome home serenade. At the appointed minute, after the ship is tied up, Liberty Call is sounded and the sailors stream down the brow to the waiting arms of their loved ones. Sometimes the reunions on the pier find the newest family members, clothed in diapers, being introduced for the first time to their fathers.

The Navy Family bronze relief was fully sponsored by the Ladies Auxiliary of the Fleet Reserve Association. Stepping aside from high technology, computerized and mass marketing fund-raising programs, the Ladies Auxiliary raised funds for their sponsorship through a variety of home-grown, tried and true programs—bake sales, raffles, sales of Lone Sailor lapel pins and tie-tacks. This dedicated group of women also played a key role in the Fleet Reserve Association's campaign to raise $1,000,000 for the Navy Memorial, including sponsorship of The Homecoming statue which stands on the Quarterdeck of the Visitors Center.

In the bronze sculpture, an aircraft carrier was chosen as the ship pulling away from its pier for and leaving for a deployment. The choice of this type of ship was at the request of the Ladies Auxiliary, who pointed out that many of the contributions came from Marine wives. They specifically asked for a carrier because it usually had a Marine contingent and sometimes an air squadron embarked. The initial concept was by naval artist CDR John Charles Roach, USNR.

A homecoming reunion following a long deployment overseas.

THE NAVY FAMILY
"They Who Wait Also Serve"
SCULPTOR: ROBERT LAMB

# U.S. Navy Supply Corps
## "Service to the Fleet"

### USS Arleigh Burke–USS Supply

GILBERT A. FRANKLIN, *Sculptor*

**F**ounded in 1795, the Supply Corps has provided responsible stewardship of the Navy's material resources, managing and guarding a supply pipeline that stretches from industrial America to storerooms and ships at sea. Logistic support of the operating forces of the Navy—that has been the fundamental job of the Navy's Supply Corps since its founding. It was formed to support six wooden frigates. And while almost everything else has changed in almost two centuries, the fundamental mission of this important Navy community has not.

A CH-46A Sea Knight helicopter lowers supplies to the deck of the amphibious assault ship *USS Tripoli* (LPH-10).

Throughout their illustrious history, the officers of the Supply Corps have kept pace with the expanding needs of the modern Navy and the scope of its mission. Supplying the Navy with over two million different items essential to the operation of modern ships, missiles, aircraft and facilities, this now specialized and highly professional community has been eminently successful in meeting the challenges of a wide range of management disciplines.

The broad responsibilities of the corps are closely related to those of many executive positions in private industry such as financial management, inventory control, merchandising, transportation, procurement, data processing, and personal services including paying and feeding personnel, and operating the Navy Exchanges and commissary stores.

In deciding upon the concept for the design, it was recognized that most of the members of the Navy supply family are ashore, ensuring that forces afloat are "Ready for Sea." The bronze relief shows a replenishment at sea by a new addition to the Navy support system, *USS Supply (AOE-6)*, resupplying one of the newest class of Navy destroyers, *USS Arleigh Burke (DDG-51)*. Seen in the rear is a "birdrep" helicopter, speeding up operations by carrying supplies by air.

The *USS Supply* is a Fast Combat Support Ship. Joining the Fleet in 1992, it can carry 150,000 barrels of oil, 1,800 tons of ammunition, 400 tons of dry stores, and 1,250 tons of refrigerated stores. The first *USS Supply* was a ship-rigged sailing vessel. It served as the supply ship for the "Black Ships" of Commodore Matthew Perry, when he opened Japan for Commerce in 1854. The ship also ferried camels to Texas in a failed attempt by then Secretary of War Jefferson Davis to use them as beasts of burden in the developing western territories of the United States.

Operating with its team of military and civilian personnel, today's Navy supply system is built on the lessons learned in war and peace on how best to support ships, overseas bases and repair activities.

The bronze relief is sponsored by the Supply Corps Association and its many friends and supporters.

U.S. NAVY SUPPLY CORPS "Service To The Fleet"
USS ARLEIGH BURKE - USS SUPPLY
SCULPTOR: GILBERT A. FRANKLIN

NAVY CHAPLAINS
"Eternal Father Strong To Save"
SCULPTOR: KLARA SEVER

# Navy Chaplains

## "Eternal Father Strong to Save"

Klara Sever, *Sculptor*

**F**or more than 200 years Navy Chaplains have worked to meet the diverse spiritual needs of the men and women of the Navy, Marine Corps, Coast Guard and Merchant Marine. The Chaplains Corps was founded on November 28, 1775, the date on which the Continental Congress adopted the second Article of Navy Regulations stating "The commanders of ships of the Thirteen United Colonies are to take care…that Divine Services are performed…" Since the nation's inception, clergy from the religious bodies of America have provided ministry to Navy people and their families. The Chaplain Corps motto "Cooperation without Compromise" is exemplified in the daily lives of chaplains, representing the myriad of faith groups, that work together administering to the members of the sea services and their families—who themselves represent the spectrum of religious beliefs in our country.

In serving all the sea services, Navy chaplains go where their people go and share their joys, hardships and dangers. The chaplain's presence takes many forms— preacher, teacher, celebrant, counselor, confessor, friend to those in need. Above all, ashore or afloat, at home or abroad, in peace or war, the chaplain's presence bears witness to Almighty God, to the faith traditions of our nation, and to the abiding nature of life's moral, spiritual and religious foundations.

As leaders in the Navy, chaplains have initiated and supported a wide range of programs to better the quality of life of the individual sea service personnel and their loved ones. Chaplains' spiritual ministry extends to family support programs, educational and counseling activities, and health and welfare concerns. Over the years, Navy chaplains have forged a proud tradition of faithfulness to God, to shipmates and their families, to the naval service, to our great nation and to each other. This legacy continues.

The sculptor, Klara Sever, was chosen because of her talent in creating religious sculptures. In her "Navy Chaplains" scene, she shows that even on a Navy combatant ship there is time for spiritual observances. Since there are more than 100 religious denominations followed by Navy and Marine personnel, she dispensed with an altar in the scene. She also wanted to include Navy and Marines, men and women. By closely examining the bronze relief, one sees that in the front row stands a Marine, while on the far left is a Navy woman in her flight suit, having just brought mail to the ship in her helicopter.

The bronze relief is sponsored by Navy Chaplains and Navy Religious Program Specialists and parishioners.

Rear Admiral Alvin B. Koeneman, CHC, USN, Chief of Chaplains, and Rear Admiral Francis L. Garrett, CHC, USN (Ret.), a former Chief of Chaplains, unveil the *Chaplain Corps* bronze relief.

# Admiral David Farragut
# Mobile Bay–1864

## "Damn the Torpedoes–Full Speed Ahead"

ROBERT SUMMERS, *Sculptor*

This famed American naval officer, who led the Union assaults on New Orleans and Mobile Bay during the Civil War, was the first United States naval leader to be advanced to the rank of Admiral. He also was among the first truly American heroes of Hispanic descent.

Admiral Farragut was born July 5, 1801 near Knoxville, Tennessee, the son of a Spanish father, George Farragut, and a North Carolinian mother, Elizabeth Shine. Young David Farragut went to sea at age eight, and earned an appointment as midshipman in the United States Navy at nine. He first saw naval combat during the War of 1812 and also took his first command when he was made prize master of a captured British ship, the *Barclay. He was 12 years old!*

Admiral Farragut's place in naval history became assured in August 1864 at the Battle of Mobile Bay, considered by some to be the most dramatic naval battle of the Civil War. As Farragut led the attack on that Confederate resupply port, the *Tecumseh* was sunk and other ships in Farragut's squadron slowed. Told that there were mines ahead—then called "torpedoes"--he ordered "Damn the torpedoes! Four bells! Captain Drayton, go ahead! Jouett, full speed!"

As seen in the bronze relief, Farragut lashed himself to the lower missen rigging of his flagship, *Hartford*, so that he could better see above smoke of the battle. During the ensuing fight, *Hartford* was struck by a glancing blow by the Confederate ironclad *Tennessee*. Maneuvering his fleet of ships through the field of mines, Farragut pressed the attack upon the defending forts.

Beyond the drama of his words and the circumstances in which they were uttered, Farragut's victory in the Battle of Mobile Bay is more significant for its strategic impact on the course of the Civil War. By closing the South's last port open to world commerce, Farragut cut off the sources of war supplies that would otherwise have flowed unimpeded in the Confederacy's overland supply routes to battlegrounds further north. It became another classic case of control of the sea—a lesson learned from ancient times to the present. Farragut, a man who once said that "the best defense is well directed fire from your own guns," learned and taught the lesson well.

A grateful nation honored the hero of Mobile Bay with the rank of four-star admiral, and some even suggested he seek the nomination for President, an accolade he declined.

Admiral David Farragut

ADMIRAL DAVID FARRAGUT – MOBILE BAY – 1864
"Damn The Torpedoes – Full Speed Ahead"
SCULPTOR: ROBERT SUMMERS

NAVAL AVIATION – FIRST SHIPBOARD TAKEOFF
Eugene Ely – Hampton Roads – 1910
SCULPTOR: GIANCARLO BIAGI

# Naval Aviation–First Shipboard Takeoff

## Eugene Ely–Hampton Roads–1910

GIANCARLO BIAGI, *Sculptor*

As the Twentieth Century dawned, not long after an Army-Navy board undertook a study of "flying machines" and envisioned their potential for use in warfare, naval aviation was born.

There was a dilemma with regard to designing the scene for the bronze sculpture honoring naval aviation. Should it be a historic scene, show the Navy's NC-4 becoming the first aircraft to fly the Atlantic, include World War II fighters? torpedo bombers? PBY patrol aircraft?—or the first carrier jets—or the jets of 1990. The decision was made to illustrate the first take-off from a ship.

The first officer selected for Navy flight training was Lieutenant T. G. Ellyson, who received orders in December 1910 to undergo instruction with Glenn Curtiss, producer of the first practical hydroplane. A month earlier, another Curtiss pilot, Eugene Ely, was the first to take off from the deck of a ship, proving that aircraft could fly from ships. In November 1910, he took off from a temporary platform built on the bow of the cruiser *USS Birmingham*, then in Hampton Roads, Virginia. Ely intended to take off while the ship was underway, but a bank of fog kept the cruiser at anchor; Ely took off anyway, as depicted in the *Naval Aviation* bronze relief. To answer the follow-on question: "Could aircraft land on ships?" Ely, in January 1911, successfully landed and took off from the battleship *USS Pennsylvania* anchored in San Francisco Bay in what could be considered the first carrier operation. Six months later, the Navy received its first airplanes, and a year after that, Lieutenant Ellyson demonstrated the feasibility of catapult launching of aircraft from ships. Naval aviation was on its way into the history books.

The Navy has taken different approaches to integrating aeronautics with the fleet—from yesteryears' flying boats and pontoon aircraft for non-carrier ships and lighter-than-air craft to today's full spectrum of carrier and land-based aircraft. Naval aviators today can pursue or support almost every possible mission faced by naval forces. Fighter planes, bombers and attack aircraft, patrol and electronic warfare aircraft, antisubmarine aircraft, cargo planes, search and rescue aircraft, helicopters—all of these comprise the naval aviation front line, a versatile and powerful extension of the sea-based aircraft carriers and battle groups that are at the heart of the U. S. Navy's effectiveness as an instrument of national policy.

The *Naval Aviation* bronze relief is sponsored by the Association of Naval Aviation.

An F6F-3 Hellcat fighter launches from *USS Yorktown* to intercept enemy forces during the "Marianas Turkey Shoot" in World War II.

# Inland Naval Engagements

## U. S. Navy River Operations–Vietnam

Serena Goldstein Litofsky, *Sculptor*

Not always on the open seas, the Navy has fought on inland waters since 1776. Most recently it was on the rivers of South Vietnam. That was the subject of this bronze sculpture, to illustrate that the Navy was active in locales other than the oceans.

In 1776, naval units on Lake Champlain under command of General Benedict Arnold, stopped a British force marching down from the St. Lawrence. If successful, the force would have threatened General Washington's army at New York. The Americans won another sea battle on Lake Champlain in 1814.

During the War of 1812, control of the Great Lakes was essential. A naval fleet was built on Lake Erie under command of the brother of Matthew C. Perry who years later opened Japan, Master Commandant Oliver Hazard Perry. Leading his forces against the British in 1813, Perry sailed in his flagship *Lawrence*, flying a banner with the words of James Lawrence, "Don't Give Up The Ship!" Following his victory on the lake, Perry sent the message: "We have met the enemy and they are ours."

The Civil War saw a "fresh water fleet" organized to gain and control the rivers. The Mississippi and other rivers including the Ohio, Tennessee and Cumberland, were scenes for combat. On the Mississippi, Admiral David Farragut, later hero of Mobile Bay, led naval forces supporting the armies of Grant and Sherman at the battle of Vicksburg.

Logos on the title plaque for the Inland Operations bronze sculpture show renderings of Oliver Hazard Perry's flagship *Lawrence* at the Battle of Lake Erie in 1813, and a Civil War river gunboat.

During the Vietnam conflict, Navy and Army units formed the Riverine Forces, while Swift boats operated off shore as well as on the rivers. *Swift Boat PCF-35*, seen in the distance in the bronze relief, was commanded by Lieutenant (junior grade) Elmo Zumwalt III, son of the U.S. Navy Commander in Vietnam (and later to become Chief of Naval Operations), Admiral Elmo Zumwalt, Jr. At the age of 39, the younger Zumwalt died of cancer believed to have been caused by Agent Orange, a defoliant used by the U. S. Armed Forces in Vietnam.

The Navy's inland war in Vietnam was part of a larger war effort in Southeast Asia involving nearly every aspect of naval operations. Other naval forces "in country" included U. S. Marines based ashore and with the Seventh Fleet Amphibious Force, the Coast Guard, the Seabees, Navy headquarters and other combat and logistic support activities. Off shore the Navy conducted carrier-based aircraft strikes in North and South Vietnam. It also had patrol aircraft and surface combatants, including the battleship *USS New Jersey* providing shore bombardment and naval gunfire support for amphibious operations, and logistic support forces—providing supplies, fuel and medical care.

The husband of sculptor Serena Litofsky served in the Vietnam conflict as an Army neurosurgeon.

Workmen place the Inland Naval Engagements on the East Sculpture Wall.

**INLAND NAVAL ENGAGEMENTS**
U.S. Navy River Operations – Vietnam
SCULPTOR: SERENA GOLDSTEIN LITOFSKY

# The Silent Service "Clean Sweep"

## WWII Submarine Patrol Returns

Stanley Bleifeld, *Sculptor*

In this bronze relief, a World War II submarine returns to Pearl Harbor displaying a broom, signifying a "clean sweep" of enemy ships from the seas. The majority of World War II submarines were of the *Gato*-class fleet submarines, although only one was in commission at the time of Pearl Harbor. But from 1942 to V-J Day, they carried the brunt of the submarine war. A little more than 300 feet in length, they had a surface speed of 21 knots, while submerged they could make ten knots. Modifications were made to submarines during the war, including addition of gun mounts. With regard to the deck gun, it is said that some skippers preferred it to be forward of the conning tower to be used in frontal attacks, some preferred it aft to ward off pursuing attackers. Some wanted two.

*USS Atlanta* is launched under a shower of colorful balloons.

A force of 288 American submarines accounted for the sinking of nearly five million tons of merchant shipping, plus 276 warships including a battleship and eight carriers. In the Pacific, the submarines were credited with sinking 54 percent of naval and commercial vessels. During the War, the Navy announced that 50 submarines were "Overdue, presumed lost." Casualties were high, reported to be six times higher than for the rest of the Navy.

Little was or could be written about the exploits of American submarines during World War II. They were the "Silent Service." They ventured right into the enemy's backyard seeking out targets or gathering intelligence. In addition to these missions, submarines rescued more than 500 allied airmen, one of whom became President of the United States, George Bush. They operated thousands of miles from homeport, many times completely alone.

The use of submersibles in warfare dates back to 1776 with the *Turtle*, used in New York harbor against the British. The first sinking of a ship by a submarine took place in the Civil War when the Confederate *Hunley* sank the Union man of war *USS Housatanic* in Charleston harbor. World War I saw the submarine emerge as a potent weapon of war.

World War II submarines were powered by diesel engines, first used by Americans in 1912. In 1954 the first nuclear powered submarine, *USS Nautilus*, was launched. A few months later she signalled "Underway on Nuclear Power."

Nuclear propulsion in submarines provided what is regarded as the first truly submersible, one which did not have to surface to recharge batteries or to draw in air for its diesels. Nuclear submarines have cruised under the polar ice pack and surfaced at the North Pole. The Triton, while submerged, circumnavigated the globe in a 41,500 mile voyage.

Today's Navy includes nuclear attack and ballistic missile submarines, the backbone of America's strategic nuclear deterrence. Nine submarines participated in Desert Storm.

The bronze sculpture was sponsored by members of the U.S. Submarine Veterans of World War II Association.

THE SILENT SERVICE "Clean Sweep"
WW II Submarine Patrol Returns
SCULPTOR STANLEY BLEIFELD

NAVAL AIRSHIPS
"They Were Dependable"
SCULPTOR: MIKLOS SIMON

# Naval Airships

## "They were dependable"

MIKLOS SIMON, *Sculptor*

I n the matter of manned flight under power, the airship precedes the fixed wing aircraft by a half century. After the first flight of a balloon with a steam engine (in France in 1852) and since World War I, the Navy's interest in rigid and non-rigid airships was for their value in scouting, anti-submarine patrol and airborne early warning.

In World War II, airships reached the peak of their use and value for the Navy. Eleven squadrons of the non-rigid or blimp type operated over the waters along North and South American, throughout the Caribbean, at the entrance to the Strait of Gibraltar, and in the Mediterranean. Three other squadrons patrolled off the U.S. west coast.

The standard patrol and escort airship for the Fleet was the ZNP-K, helium-inflated, with a length of 252 feet. The *Naval Airships* sculpture depicts a convoy scene as viewed from the cockpit of one of these blimps. The pilot mans the elevator wheel while an enlisted crew member takes his turn on the rudder wheel. "K-ships" normally carried four officers and six enlisted men. Some enlisted were qualified as Aviation Pilots.

Atlantic Fleet airships flew 378,237 hours in 37,554 flights and escorted more than 70,000 surface ship voyages. In the Pacific their record was 167,291 hours, 20,156 flights and 11,000 surface ships escorted. In the Atlantic, U.S. Navy blimps made numerous antisubmarine attacks, and one of them, the K-74, was shot down by a surfaced U-boat.

The wartime build-up in Lighter-than-Air, as the Navy's airship program was known, amounted to more than 160 blimps, 1500 pilots and 3000 aircrewmen. Their most historic flights were the eight made from the United States to Port Lyautey, French Morocco, the first ocean crossings by non-rigid airships.

The blimps of World War II were the descendants of those flown by the Navy during World War I and in the years between the wars. They were the successors to the large rigid airships—the *Shenandoah, Los Angeles, Akron* and *Macon*—which the Navy abandoned in 1935.

New and larger blimps followed after World War II, including some for Airborne Early Warning use. In 1961 Lighter-than-Air was officially ordered terminated, ending a branch of the naval service that had begun in 1917. The last flight by a U.S. Navy airship took place August 13, 1962.

Their wartime mission was threefold—anti-submarine warfare, anti-mine warfare and search and rescue. It has been said that if airships had served no other function in the war, their record of locating and rescuing shipwrecked and air wrecked crews merits them national gratitude.

While the airships served, "they were dependable."

The bronze relief is sponsored by the Naval Airships Association.

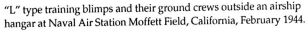
"L" type training blimps and their ground crews outside an airship hangar at Naval Air Station Moffett Field, California, February 1944.

# Navy Medicine

## "Standing By to Assist"

ANTONIO TOBIAS MENDEZ, *Sculptor*

**P**ictured in the bronze relief is a scene on the deck of a Navy hospital ship off the coast of Korea during that conflict. A Navy doctor and Navy nurse are attending a patient brought by a medical evacuation helicopter. Two Navy Hospital Corpsmen ready an *I.V.*, while two others watch the helicopter depart.

In 1775, the first American naval surgeon, Joseph Harrison, was aboard *Alfred* when John Paul Jones hoisted the first American flag to fly from a warship. The Navy's Medical Department was founded in 1842. Today, Navy Medicine encompasses a community of 55,000 Navy medical personnel, including 43,000 uniformed caregivers—nearly 4,300 medical corps, 3,100 nurse corps, 2,800 medical service corps, 1,700 dental corps, 27,700 hospital corpsmen, 3,400 dental technicians and 12,000 civilians. These dedicated, highly skilled professionals provide care for nearly 786,000 active duty Navy and Marine Corps personnel, 886,000 dependents and Navy and Marine Corps retirees and their dependents or survivors numbering 1,126,600—a total beneficiary population of almost 3,000,000 people.

Nearly one-fourth of the Navy's health care providers are assigned to afloat units—ships, squadrons or afloat staffs—and to deployable units of the Marine Corps. The mission of these and their shorebased compatriots is much the same as when the Navy's medical community was founded—to be operationally ready to meet wartime medical requirements and provide quality care to active duty military, the families and retirees.

In 1992, Navy Medicine operated 33 hospitals, 213 medical clinics, 168 dental clinics and five drug screening laboratories. In addition, the community includes a research and development command, which has medical and dental health research institutes, units and laboratories. The community has its own health sciences education and training command which operates four schools. A Medical Corps vice admiral is the senior medical authority for the Navy and serves on the staff of the Chief of Naval Operations. As the Navy's Surgeon General and Chief of the Bureau of Medicine and Surgery, this officer is in charge of setting and implementing medical policy for the Navy and Marine Corps.

In war and peace, Navy Medicine has compiled a glorious record of achievements. During the twentieth century, 27 members of the community have been recognized for their heroism through awards of the Congressional Medal of Honor. Thousands more have been honored by their medical peers for extraordinary achievements in medical research and medical care, in the detection, treatment and prevention of disease, in extending the frontiers of outer space and the inner space of ocean depths, in improving occupational and environmental safety for naval personnel, and in enhancing combat readiness of the Navy.

The bronze relief is sponsored by members of the Navy Medical Family. In addition, the American Medical Association, the American Hospital Association, Hoechst-Roussel Pharmaceuticals, and Glaxo, Inc. contributed to the Navy Memorial Foundation toward the sponsorship of this bronze relief.

Vice Admiral James A. Zimble, MC, USN, sculptor Antonio Tobias Mendez, Rear Admiral William Thompson, USN (Ret.), and Vice Admiral Donald F. Hagen, MC, USN, at the *Navy Medicine* bronze relief dedication ceremony, which featured the U. S. Navy Band's Sea Chanters (in background).

NAVY MEDICINE
"Standing By To Assist"
SCULPTOR: ANTONIO TOBIAS MENDEZ

# Naval Reservists

## "Twice a Citizen"

LEO C. IRRERA, *Sculptor*

The U.S. Naval Reserve was not formally established until March 3, 1915, but the concept of citizen sailors is as old as our nation. Thomas Jefferson suggested the creation of a Naval Militia as early as 1805, and various states established Naval Militia or similar "citizen-sailor" units, some of which augmented the Navy in both the Civil War and the Spanish-American War. By the end of World War I, there were 330,000 Naval Reserve personnel on active duty, including 12,000 women Yeoman (F).

In World War II, four of every five persons who served in the Navy were reservists. After the war, a number of them remained in the Naval Reserve's cadre of approximately 130,000 drilling reservists. Many of these individuals were recalled to active duty for the Korean War. Approximately 75 percent of Navy combat sorties were flown by reserve aviators during that conflict. In 1967, during the war in Vietnam, nearly one of seven Navymen and women on active duty was a reservist.

In recent years, the Naval Reserve has begun to assume some operational responsibilities. During 1987, when regional hostilities intensified in the Persian Gulf, deployed Naval Reserve Force (NRF) minesweepers were continuously on station under Operation Earnest Will to augment airborne mine countermeasures and explosive ordnance disposal units already on the scene.

During 1990-91 for Operation Desert Shield and Desert Storm, 21,109 Naval Reservists were called to active duty. Their highly successful deployment validated the Defense Department "total force" policy in which reservists train to maintain skills vital to perform wartime military missions to supplement the active force.

The primary mission of the Naval Reserve is to provide trained units and qualified individuals available for active duty in time of war or national emergency or to supplement the peacetime needs of the active forces. Training missions are devoted whenever possible to provide maximum contributory support to active commands and to maintain readiness of reserve personnel for active service at the highest levels possible.

The "total force" of the Navy embraces all of its assets—people and hardware. As a result, Naval Reserve strength is directly related to the inventory of ships, aircraft and support equipment. Wherever they may be, drilling at Reserve Centers all over the country or on active duty for training on the high seas, Naval reservists are full partners with the active Navy.

Privateers, naval militia and naval reservists—by whatever names—have faithfully served and continue to serve our nation with honor, pride and distinction during peace and war.

In their civilian roles, out of uniform, reservists fulfill their life's work in the mainstreams of America's economy and society. But they are always ready, as depicted in sculptor Leo C. Irrera's bronze relief, to leave the civilian world behind and don the uniforms, obligations and sacrifices of active service in the Navy. In this regard they are in all respects "twice a citizen."

The bronze relief is sponsored by the Naval Reserve Association with assistance from the Naval Enlisted Reserve Association.

Navy Memorial's sculptor coordinator Leo C. Irrera with the *Naval Reservists* bronze relief, one of three he created for the Memorial.

NAVAL RESERVISTS
"Twice A Citizen"
SCULPTOR: LEO C. IRRERA

USNR

LEO IRRERA

# Women in the Navy

## On Shore, In the Air and At Sea

SERENA GOLDSTEIN LITOFSKY, *Sculptor*

W omen began their service in the Navy as nurses in 1908, adding new chapters as the Yeoman (F) of World War I, the *WAVES* of World War II, and today's women in the Navy who serve their country as part of the Navy team—on shore, in the air, and on ships at sea.

It was in World War I that women's role in the Navy first came into its own—while leaving a long way to go. The Navy Nurse Corps was born in 1908, and in addition to the nurses, some 12,000 women served on active duty as "yeomanettes." They were the answer to Secretary of the Navy Josephus Daniels' question, "Is there any law that says a yeoman has to be a man?" Ever since, in a long and glorious saga of service, women of the Navy have been building traditions of excellence while tearing down antiquated traditions about their place and the role of women in the military.

In July 1942, President Franklin D. Roosevelt signed the legislation authorizing the enlistment and commissioning of women in the Naval Reserve—the first time women were allowed to be part of the armed services instead of an auxiliary to a service branch. Thus was born the WAVES— Women Accepted for Volunteer Emergency Service. More progress was to be made during and following World War II, when women—previously confined to reserve status— were at last permitted to become a part of the Regular Navy. In the next four decades, women's opportunities continued to expand, including assignments to and in command of ships and air squadrons of the Navy—and promotion to flag rank in the unrestricted line officer corps.

Women in the Navy today serve side by side their male counterparts in almost every aspect of naval service, as depicted by Sculptor Serena Goldstein Litofsky's bronze relief. To develop the concept for the sculpture, Mrs. Litofsky went on board Navy ships, including one in which 40 percent of the crew were Navy women. Using the hundreds of photographs which were taken, she developed the scene of a bridge on a ship underway. Women and men are integrated into a team.

It was not possible in a single scene to cover the history and diversified background of women in the Navy, past and present. But the sculpture does capture the essence of women's service in a depiction that the American public can identify as quintessentially Navy, namely, service at sea on board ship.

This work was sponsored by the Navy Women National Convention Association and the Women Officer's Professional Association. The sculpture was the first of the 22 panels on the sculpture wall to be fully sponsored, and was dedicated on the Navy's birthday in October 1990.

*WAVE* mechanics working on the engine of a Naval Air Transport Service Douglas R5D aircraft in 1945.

THE GREAT WHITE FLEET – 1907
"Speak Softly And Carry A Big Stick"
SCULPTOR: GILBERT A. FRANKLIN

# The Great White Fleet–1907

## "Speak softly and carry a big stick"

GILBERT A. FRANKLIN, *Sculptor*

F resh on the heels of mediating the peace talks in the Russo-Japanese War and becoming the first American to win the Nobel Peace Prize, President Theodore Roosevelt decided to display to the world America's newly acquired naval strength and to establish the United States as a world power.

Prior to the Spanish-American War, Roosevelt had been Assistant Secretary of the Navy. So he was well acquainted with the state of the fleet when he became President in 1901. He immediately pushed Congress to authorize two battleships per year. In 1907, he sent the entire U.S. Navy Battle Fleet on a good-will tour around the world—16 battleships, brightly painted in white. All had been built since the Spanish-American War. Accompanying the battle line were auxiliaries and coaling ships.

As shown in the bronze relief, when the Great White Fleet sailed from Hampton Roads, Virginia, on December 16, 1907, Roosevelt reviewed the departure of the Fleet from the presidential yacht *Mayflower*.

The ships sailed south through the Atlantic, around Cape Horn and up the west coast of the South American continent. In every port they were warmly greeted. Sailing north they called at San Francisco. Going west to Hawaii,

they crossed the Pacific, calling at ports in Australia, the Philippines, China and Japan. They cruised on across the Indian Ocean, made a transit of the Suez Canal, sailed through the Mediterranean, and returned across the Atlantic to Hampton Roads in February 1909.

The fleet was at sea for 14 months and steamed 46,000 miles, the longest voyage yet for the relatively new technology of steam-powered steel battleships. Roosevelt had insisted that the Navy stay highly efficient. This state of readiness paid off during the world cruise, which established that the Navy could operate at sea, steaming long distances, far from home ports. The whole world was impressed.

"Speak softly and carry a big stick; you will go far," said President Roosevelt. "If the American nation will speak softly, and yet build and keep at a pitch of the highest training a thoroughly efficient Navy, the Monroe Doctrine will go far."

Commenting on his "big stick" diplomacy, Roosevelt declared that it "was the most important service (he) rendered to peace."

The Great White Fleet bronze relief is sponsored by the Naval Order of the United States.

"The Great White Fleet," led by battleships *USS Kansas (BB-21)* and *USS Vermont (BB-22)*, begins its 'round the world voyage steaming out of Hampton Roads, Virginia, in December 1907.

# Navy Astronauts and Recovery Missions

## A Contribution to U.S. Space Age

ROBERT SUMMERS, *Sculptor*

The first American in outer space, in May 1961, was a naval aviator and astronaut, Commander Alan B. Shepard, Jr., now a retired rear admiral and member of the Navy Memorial Foundation's Board of Directors. He is the first in a long succession of naval aviators to enter America's space program—including Marine Corps pilot John Glenn, the first American to orbit the earth (February 1962), and former Navy pilot Astronaut Neil Armstrong, the first person to set foot on the moon (July 1969). Four of the original Mercury Seven had been designated naval aviators.

Shepard's first flight in space lasted 15 minutes, reached a height of 115 miles and a speed of 5,290 mph, and landed 320 miles down course in the Atlantic. He later was part of Apollo 14 and set foot on the moon in early 1971. In a video of the landing, he is seen swinging a golf club, the first to do so in a non-gravity environment.

As the program developed, other naval aviators became astronauts and part of space exploration—James A. Lovell, Eugene A. Cernan and Richard F. Gordon, Jr. were in the Gemini program. Lovell and Cernan became part of the Apollo lunar program, joining naval aviators Charles Conrad, Jr., Alan L. Bean, Richard F. Cordor, Jr., John W.

Young (also first space shuttle commander), Roland E. Evans and Edgar D. Mitchell, as well as Air Force officers and civilians.

As with all "splash downs" in the ocean, from Mercury to Apollo, well rehearsed naval forces were on hand to pluck the astronaut and to retrieve the space capsule from the seas. Conducted under the National Aeronautics and Space Administration, all U. S. manned space flights — until the advent of today's shuttle missions— wound up in the hands of U. S. Navy recovery forces at sea, as portrayed in this bronze relief. On many occasions Navy frogmen attached flotation collars to the spacecraft. Ships, small boats and helicopters, as depicted in the sculpture, then airlifted the astronauts to nearby ships.

The capsules parachuted to earth, usually in close proximity to the waiting ships. However, Commander Carpenter's Mercury flight overshot the landing area, coming down 240 miles away. A Navy search aircraft homed in on a radio beacon and found the astronaut in a rubber life raft alongside his capsule.

Robert Summers, of Glen Rose, Texas, in doing research for his sculpture, conferred with Rear Admiral Shepard, also a Texan living in Houston.

The Apollo 13 command module is craned aboard the recovery ship *USS Iwo Jima (LPH-2)* on April 17, 1970.

NAVY ASTRONAUTS AND RECOVERY MISSIONS
A Contribution To The U.S. Space Age
SCULPTOR ROBERT SUMMERS

**UNITED STATES MARINE CORPS**

Amphibious Assault – Inchon – 1950

SCULPTOR: FRED PRESS

# United States Marine Corps

## Amphibious Assault–Inchon 1950

FRED PRESS, *Sculptor*

U nlike other amphibious landings across beaches characteristic of World War II, the amphibious landing at Inchon, Korea, presented a unique set of circumstances—extreme tidal variations, swift currents and the obstruction of a high sea wall for the Marines to scale while under fire. According to one correspondent, the sea wall seemed "as high as the RCA building." Another wrote that the incoming amphibious craft, with their scaling ladders sticking up, looked like some sort of insects with their antennas rigid. Only a few hours on a few days lent themselves to carrying out an amphibious assault. Some 230 ships participated in the operation in September 1950. Initial attacks were against an Inchon harbor fortress, Wolmi-do, seen in the background on the bronze relief.

After the operation, Fleet Admiral William F. Halsey called it "the most masterly and audacious strategic stroke in all history." General Douglas MacArthur, commander in chief in the Far East, who witnessed the landing from the flagship *Mount McKinley*, exclaimed: "The Navy and the Marines have never shone more brightly."

Almost every major offensive campaign the United States launched during World War II was initiated by an amphibious assault, as were the principal offensives of the Korean War. Marines and amphibious warfare go together, the melding of the Navy-Marine Corps Team.

Amphibious warfare integrates virtually all types of ships, aircraft, weapons and landing forces in a concerted military effort against a hostile shore; one of the most potent of these resources is the Marines.

The Marine Corps dates from the resolution of the Continental Congress on November 10, 1775, authorizing two battalions of Marines. The Marines served gallantly throughout the revolution, as they have throughout America's history—"From the halls of Montezuma, to the shores of Tripoli," on land, on sea and in the air, in wartime and peacetime. The story of World War II in the Pacific cannot be told without major dependence on the glorious record of the Marines—Guadalcanal, Tarawa, the Marshalls, the Marianas, the Palaus and finally, Iwo Jima, where "uncommon valor was a common virtue." In Korea, the Inchon landing depicted in the bronze relief was a pivotal point in the war, enabling the United Nations forces to shift from a defensive posture to an offensive one. The Navy-Marine assault forced the enemy North Korean armies to withdraw rapidly northward. In Vietnam, Marines compiled a distinguished record in combat both in amphibious operations and sustained operations ashore. Most recently, the Marines were engaged in combat in the Persian Gulf, for the liberation of Kuwait.

The relief is sponsored by United States Marines, with a contribution from Waste Management Corporation.

Fourth Marine Division moving up the beach of Iwo Jima on D-Day, February 19, 1945. Making their fourth amphibious assault in 13 months, the veteran fighters are ready to secure the right flank on the initial beachhead. An "LSM" is in the background.

# United States Coast Guard

## Semper Paratus–"Always Ready"

ROBERT SUMMERS, *Sculptor*

T he United States Coast Guard was founded on August 4, 1790, by Alexander Hamilton to combat smuggling. It has a dual role that is unique among the services. By statute, organization and operation, the Coast Guard normally operates as part of the Department of Transportation. In time of war or when the President so directs, it operates under control of the Navy. Regardless, it is truly a sea service, and one that has maintained a tradition of professional excellence and dedicated service for more than 200 years.

The Coast Guard fulfills three primary missions: defense readiness, maritime safety and maritime law enforcement. The service operates ships, specialized vessels, rotary and fixed-wing aircraft, research and development facilities and shore installations. The distinctive white hulls of Coast Guard vessels, carrying the unique slash-stripes on the bows, are instantly recognized.

Considering that the bronze sculpture honoring the United States Coast Guard was to be installed at the Navy Memorial, one thought was that its scene should show the Coast Guard operating with the Navy. But there was the question, usually during combat all ships are painted grey, so how could one tell a Coast Guard ship from a Navy one. Further, and as finally depicted in this bronze relief, the Coast Guard is renowned for its rescues at sea of civilian sailors and recreational boaters in distress. So that was the scene chosen.

The Coast Guard also is the licensing and safety certification authority for the operation of all but the smallest of boats. Likewise, it periodically inspects U.S. merchant vessels. It is also known for its aggressive role in the war on drugs and for disaster relief. The Coast Guard establishes and maintains America's aids to navigation such as lighthouses, radio beacons, buoys and other markers in the channels and sea lanes of bays and rivers. It assists marine commerce by opening ice-blocked channels and ports, and it is engaged in the prevention and cleanup of pollution and the protection of U. S. fisheries.

The Coast Guard operates throughout the world. Working with naval units, it formed boarding parties which were active during the 1962 Cuban missile crisis and during and after Desert Storm, inspecting suspect ships in the Persian Gulf.

Peacetime missions have seen the Coast Guard participating in Operation Deep Freeze in the Antarctic. And it operates ice breakers, carrying out icebreaking services in the Great Lakes, Alaskan waters, as well as in the Arctic and Antarctic regions. In 1992, 37,000 officers and enlisted personnel served in the Coast Guard.

Sponsored by past and present members of the United States Coast Guard, with contributions from the Coast Guard Chief Petty Officers Association, General Electric, Arco Marine Inc. and Sea-Land Service Inc.

U. S. Coast Guard patrol boat *Matagorda* on patrol in the Caribbean.

UNITED STATES COAST GUARD
Semper Paratus – "Always Ready"
SCULPTOR·ROBERT·SUMMERS

EXPLORATION, OCEANOGRAPHY, RESEARCH
Navy Lieutenant Charles Wilkes In Antarctic – 1840
SCULPTOR: ANTONIO TOBIAS MENDEZ

# Exploration, Oceanography, Research

## Navy Lieutenant Charles Wilkes in Antarctica–1840

ANTONIO TOBIAS MENDEZ, *Sculptor*

Throughout America's history, the U. S. Navy has played a significant role, including leadership, in scientific research and exploration. The role is exemplified in this bronze relief depicting one of the Navy's earliest research ventures. In 1828, President John Quincy Adams suggested a coastal exploration of the northwest frontier to add to knowledge gained by the Lewis and Clark expedition. This led, ten years later, to the U.S. Exploring Expedition of 1838-1842.

It was led by Navy Lieutenant Charles Wilkes, selected not for his rank, but more for his scientific background as director of the Depot of Charts and Instruments (later the Naval Observatory). Naval scientists in hydrography, mapping and magnetic and astronomical observations joined civilian scientists on the expedition. Together they explored some 1,500 miles of Antarctic coastlines, proving the existence of a seventh continent. The Navy remained in the forefront of polar exploration, both at the North Pole, overflown by Rear Admiral Richard E. Byrd in 1926, and later, Operation Deep Freeze in the Antarctic.

Wilkes' expedition brought back valuable knowledge in many of the sciences. His surveys of Pacific Islands resulted in creation of many navigational charts, including those used by the Navy in 1943 at Tarawa.

Spurred on by the success of the Wilkes mission, the Navy was active in further overseas exploration. Naval officers led expeditions to West Africa, the Middle East, Central and South America, the China Sea and Japan, and the North Pacific Ocean. During the period 1869–1874, the Navy conducted several surveys of the Central America isthmus in order to examine possible routes for a canal between the Atlantic and Pacific oceans. The surveys gathered enough information to determine the best route from an engineering standpoint.

About the middle of the nineteenth century, the Navy established its first testing laboratories to keep pace with civilian inventions and general progress of technology. In 1923, the Navy opened the Naval Research Laboratory (NRL) in Washington.

NRL was the first U.S. government agency to study atomic power. The world's first high speed digital computer was developed by scientists supported by the organization that became the Office of Naval Research. The Navy was instrumental in the development of

Aquanauts work to attach umbilical lines from a support ship to the Sealab III undersea habitat during one phase of the research project in December 1968.

fiberglass and sandwich wrapping material—which resulted from research for thin, plastic balloons to study the upper atmosphere. The development of the transistor and all the related marvels of the electronics industry are the products of basic research in solid state physics supported in a large part by the Navy. Navy research also led to design of the lithium dry cell battery.

The Navy continues today to operate a comprehensive system for research, development, test and evaluation across a wide range of scientific disciplines.

U.S. MERCHANT MARINE – U.S. NAVY ARMED GUARD
"We Deliver"

SCULPTOR: ROBERT LAMB

# U.S. Merchant Marine–
# U.S. Navy Armed Guard

## "We deliver"

Robert Lamb, *Sculptor*

A nation's merchant ships are an important part of her sea power, especially so in time of war when they provide the vital link between the fighting force overseas and the industrial output on the home front. In both world wars the Merchant Marine/Navy Armed Guard team met the challenge and delivered.

Shown in this bronze relief is a convoy under attack while enroute to Murmansk during World War II; though manned by civilian crews, the ships carried gun crews of Navy gunners—the U. S. Navy Armed Guard. "The run to Murmansk" across the north Atlantic and through the Norwegian and Barents seas was the most direct logistic link between America and the USSR, then struggling for survival against Nazi Germany. The voyage combined all the elements of danger from man and nature alike.

During the war, more than 700 American merchantmen of over 1,000 gross tons were victims of enemy operations or marine disasters. During a typical month in 1942 and 1943, over 50 allied merchant ships were lost in the North Atlantic. On the Murmansk run, 63 vessels were lost. The combat casualties at sea resulted in the deaths of more than 1,800 U.S. Navy Armed Guard members, nearly 6,200 U.S. merchant marine seamen and 529 members of the Army Transport Service.

Throughout the war, wherever convoys sailed, the slow, gray ships and brave crews were exposed to attack by dive bombers, surface raiders and submarines. The U. S. Navy Armed Guard contingents formed each ship's only on-board protection against the enemy; the gun crews were often augmented by merchant seamen from the ships' crews. Despite significant opposition by a determined enemy, the teams worked together to deliver the cargoes to our deployed forces.

The Armed Guard was formed prior to the attack on Pearl Harbor. An Armed Guard School at Little Creek, Virginia, was established in October 1941, and the first graduates reported for duty just as the authority was granted to place guns on merchant ships to protect them from attack. Nearly 150,000 Navy men served in the Armed Guard during World War II.

Sculptor Robert Lamb is a U.S. Merchant Marine

The clay rendering of sculptor Robert Lamb's *Merchant Marine/Armed Guard* bronze relief.

Academy graduate and a veteran of World War II's Murmansk convoys. However, to work on the sculpture he needed photographs for reference because as an engineering officer below decks, he did not witness the battles going on topside.

This bronze relief was made possible by contributions from the Seafarers International Union, alumni of the U.S. Merchant Marine Academy and the state merchant marine academies, and by veterans of the Merchant Marine, as well as the U.S. Navy Armed Guard Association.

# United States Naval Academy

## Ex Scientia Tridens–"From knowledge, sea power"

MIKLOS SIMON, *Sculptor*

The role of the Naval Academy is to educate and train young men and women to become officers in the United States Navy and the Marine Corps. The Naval Academy aims to develop midshipmen morally, mentally and physically, and to imbue them with the highest ideals of duty, honor and loyalty—enabling them to be professional officers in the naval service and to progress to the highest responsibilities of command, citizenship and government.

President John Quincy Adams was an advocate of government support of scientific enterprise and encouraged official military participation in it. One of his proposals, eventually accepted, led to the establishment of the United States Naval Academy, where half of its curriculum was devoted to science and engineering. In 1845, George Bancroft, Secretary of the Navy under President James K. Polk, founded the Naval Academy in Annapolis, Maryland.

The concept for the Naval Academy bronze sculpture was developed with several objectives. One is to show that the Academy has both a military and an academic function, thus midshipmen are seen marching in formation, as well as more informally proceeding to classes. The sculpture also had to show that both women and men form the Academy's student body, women having been first admitted in 1976. In the background of the sculpture is Bancroft Hall, the "dorm" for all the midshipmen, while in the foreground is the back of the statue *Tecumseh*.

More than 1,000 men and women enter the Naval Academy each year. Candidates for appointment as midshipmen must meet high physical, academic and moral standards. The Academy offers 18 majors in engineering, science and mathematics, and humanities and social science. Technical areas are stressed in the curriculum, as well as humanities, naval science, physical conditioning and leadership. After four years of rigorous studies, graduates are awarded Bachelor of Science degrees and their commissions during graduation week; for one such graduation, in 1907, the song "Anchors Aweigh" was composed.

Academy graduates continue to distinguish themselves in military roles as well as in corporate and public life. President Jimmy Carter, Class of 1947, was the first Academy graduate to hold the highest office in the land.

An hour's drive from the Navy Memorial, the United States Naval Academy covers some 322 acres on the banks of the Severn River in Annapolis, the state capital of Maryland.

The bronze relief is sponsored by the United States Naval Academy Alumni Association.

The U. S. Naval Academy, Annapolis, Maryland.

UNITED STATES NAVAL ACADEMY – ANNAPOLIS
Ex Scientia Tridens – "From Knowledge, Sea Power"
SCULPTOR: MIKLOS SIMON

# Destroyer Escorts

## "Trim but deadly"

GILBERT A. FRANKLIN, *Sculptor*

**D**estroyer Escorts (DE) were famed as convoy defenders and multi-purpose ships. They sank submarines, battled kamikazes, supported amphibious operations and rescued aviators and sailors.

The bronze relief commemorating these ships and their crews was the first to be dedicated at the Navy Memorial, on September 1, 1990. For the occasion, President George Bush sent greetings:

" . . . The brave Americans and the swift, highly maneuverable vessels memorialized by this plaque have earned a special place of honor in American naval history. Those who served aboard Destroyer Escorts during World War II were part of a generation that was called to defend our way of life against the forces of tyranny and aggression. DE crews fought courageously to protect the lifeline of ships that supplied the arsenal of freedom. Sinking enemy submarines, battling kamikazes, and rescuing downed aviators and sailors in distress, they played a pivotal role in the war at sea and contributed to the Allied victory.

"The plaque will be a lasting testament to the dedication and sacrifice of the DE Sailor—not only those who served during World War II but also those who carried on their outstanding legacy in Korea and Vietnam.

It will serve as a poignant reminder of the great debt we owe to all the men and women of our Nation's seafaring services . . . I applaud the spirit of the DE Sailor."

The creation of the DE in 1942 was an historic event, born of necessity and produced in quantity—and example of American ingenuity and production capability. Manned almost entirely by Naval Reservists, the DEs were commanded by the likes of W. Graham Claytor, former Secretary of the Navy and now president of Amtrak, and the late football coaching great "Woody" Hayes.

The multi-purpose ships of World War II, Korea and Vietnam—destroyer escorts ranged between 1,140 and 1,450 tons, about 300 feet long with a 35-foot beam, capable of 20 to 24 knots, and had between 200 and 225 crewmen. Approximately 600 destroyer escorts were built, most of them on crash schedules of 90 days. There were several variations of DEs, some with 3"50 guns, some with 5"38s. The first DEs built were named after destroyers which had been lost in 1941 and 1942.

Some 150,000 Navy men have served in these versatile ships, earning for themselves the proud distinction of Destroyer Escort Sailors. They evince this pride in their sponsorship of their bronze relief by sculptor Gilbert A. Franklin through the Destroyer Escort Sailors Association.

Destroyer Escort Association officer John Cosgrove speaking at the September 1, 1990 dedication of the Destroyer Escort bronze relief.

DESTROYER ESCORTS
"Trim But Deadly"
SCULPTOR: GILBERT A. FRANKLIN

OPENING JAPAN FOR COMMERCE
Commodore Matthew Perry – 1854
SCULPTOR: LEO C. IRRERA

# Opening Japan for Commerce
## Commodore Matthew Perry–1854

Leo C. Irrera, *Sculptor*

**O**ut of mistrust of missionaries and foreign traders, Japan had been by its own choice a hermit country, cut off from the outside world for more than two centuries. Foreigners were not welcome and Japanese could not leave their country. Sailors, including Americans, visited the waters off Japan in search of whales. In uncharted waters, ships were often wrecked and those on board taken into custody.

U. S. government concern prompted the mission of Commodore Matthew C. Perry who was well suited for the assignment. Early in his career he had carried out diplomatic missions in African and Mediterranean waters. He was well known in European court circles and the Czar of Russia once offered to make him an admiral in the Russian Navy.

Perry was ordered to open diplomatic and trade relations with Japan and ensure the safety of shipwrecked American sailors. The State Department gave him free hand and Perry undertook the duty seriously, spending two years to study Japan. Perry reasoned that others before him had failed because they tried to deal with the Japanese using western tactics. He found that the Japanese of that era were fond of ceremony, formality and pomp.

While his primary mission was to make Japan safe for shipwrecked sailors, he also aimed to conclude treaties which would open Japan for commerce. He sailed into Tokyo Bay on July 8, 1853, to lay the groundwork for a return visit the following year.

Considering that the Japanese had fired on the ships of other nations attempting such visits, Perry evidently impressed the Japanese with his show of force and dignity. It was a mission that demanded exceptional diplomacy. The commodore's philosophy was to adopt two extremes "... by an exhibition of great pomp, when it could properly be displayed, and by avoiding it, when such pomp would be inconsistent with the spirit of our institutions." After initial engagements with the Japanese, Perry left for six months.

When Perry made his second visit, in March 1854, the Japanese were waiting with a red carpet welcome. They were ready to extend hospitality to American sailors and to sign a trade treaty—a treaty which opened for American trade the ports of Hakodate and Shimoda.

The bronze sculpture shows Commodore Perry being greeted by Japanese diplomats. It is said that many Japanese came from surrounding areas to witness the arrival of Perry's "black ships," so called because of the black smoke pouring out their stacks. Perry's ships are seen in the background. Today in Shimoda, the Japanese and the U. S. Seventh Fleet annually celebrate the Black Ship Festival.

Americans and Japanese, including a delegation dressed as Commodore Perry's party, enjoy the Black Ship Festival in Shimoda, Japan.

# Captain John Paul Jones

## "... In Harm's Way"

FRED PRESS, *Sculptor*

John Paul Jones emerged from the Revolutionary War as one of the Navy's greatest heroes and tradition makers. None of these traditions stands out more conspicuously than his refusal to acknowledge defeat, even against overwhelming odds: "I have not yet begun to fight," he replied, when asked to surrender his ship *Bonhomme Richard*. With this indomitable resolve, the spirit of the U. S. Navy is embodied in John Paul Jones.

In 1775 the Continental Congress founded the American Navy which faced a formidable foe in the mighty and usually invincible Royal Navy. It acquitted itself surprisingly well and by the end of 1777 had captured 464 British vessels. That year, as a reward for his accomplishments in *Providence* and *Alfred*, Captain John Paul Jones was given command of the 18-gun sloop of war *Ranger*. On February 14, 1778, in Quiberon Bay, France, the flagship of a French fleet fired a salute to *Ranger*—the first salute to the Stars and Stripes by a foreign warship.

Two months later *Ranger* defeated *HMS Drake* in the Irish Sea, which battle is depicted in the bronze relief by sculptor Fred Press. Later, in anticipation of yet another command, Jones set forth his specifications, "I wish to have no connection with any ship that does not sail fast, for I intend to go in harm's way."

John Paul Jones was born in Scotland and was originally named John Paul. However, after killing a mutinous crewman on board a merchantman, he fled to America and adopted the name Jones. He received a lieutenant's commission in the Continental Navy in 1775, a year before being given command of *Providence*.

The battle in 1779 of the British *Serapis* against *Bonhomme Richard* was the last big sea engagement fought by the American Continental Navy. *Serapis*, when engaged, was escorting British merchantmen off Flamborough Head on the English coast. She was a new frigate carrying 50 guns. *Bonhomme Richard* had been an old East Indian merchantman named *Duc de Duras*. Jones rebuilt her into a warship, and christened her *Bonhomme Richard*, after Poor Richard's Almanac, published by his friend Benjamin Franklin.. Although outmanned and outgunned, Jones prevailed and the *Serapis* struck her colors. Jones captured her, and the *Bonhomme Richard* sank two days after the battle. Following his victory with *Bonhomme Richard*, he never again held a major American sea command. In 1788, he was appointed a Rear Admiral in the Russian Navy by Empress Catherine II. He lived in Paris until his death. His body was returned to the United States and lies in a crypt under the Naval Academy chapel.

The relief is made possible by Robert E. Naser, president of Robert E. Naser Realty and a member of the Navy Memorial Foundation Board of Directors.

Detail from sculptor Fred Press' rendering of *John Paul Jones*.

CAPTAIN JOHN PAUL JONES
*".... In Harm's Way"*
SCULPTOR: FRED PRESS

# The Sculptors

GIANCARLO BIAGI, sculptor of the Naval Aviation bronze relief, was born in Vesilia of Tuscany, Italy, in 1952. He studied with the Art Institute of Stagio Stagi and the Tommasi Foundry in Pietrasanta, Italy, the Art Student's League and Lester Polakov Set Design, both in New York. Mr. Biagi's works appear in the collections of several Italian museums, the City Hall of Seravezza, Italy and the Trondelag Theatre, Norway, and have appeared in more than 20 exhibitions throughout Europe and the United States. He is the recipient of numerous awards and grants. Mr. Biagi maintains studios in Pietrasanta and New York.

STANLEY BLEIFELD, sculptor of the Silent Service bronze relief, is also the sculptor of the Lone Sailor statue on the Memorial plaza map of the world and The Homecoming statue in the Quarterdeck lobby of the Visitors Center. A native of Brooklyn, New York and a Navy veteran of World War II, Mr. Bleifeld received his formal education including a Master of Fine Arts degree from The Tyler School of Fine Art, Temple University, Philadelphia. His works have been exhibited and are part of a dozen gallery and library collections throughout America. This award-winning sculptor was most recently honored by the National Sculpture Society with its prestigious Henry Hering Memorial Medal, for his sculpture work on the Lone Sailor. Mr. Bleifeld works from his studios in Weston, Connecticut, and Pietrasanta, Italy.

Waters "salted" from samples of the Seven Seas of the world tumble down a seven-step cascade on the Memorial's corner pools.

GILBERT A. FRANKLIN, sculptor of the bronze reliefs honoring Destroyer Escorts and the Navy Supply Corps and commemorating the historic voyage of the Great White Fleet, studied at the Rhode Island School of Design (RISD), the American Academy in Rome and Museo Nacional, Mexico City. The principal artist or participant in numerous one-man and group shows, Mr. Franklin has earned numerous awards and public commissions, and his works appear in a number of collections throughout the eastern U. S.; he is a recipient of the *Prix de Rome*. He has been an art critic, Dean of Fine Arts at RISD, visiting lecturer, teacher and artist-in-residence at Harvard, Yale, Maryland Art Institute, American Academy in Rome, University of Pennsylvania, Dartmouth and others. He resides in Wellfleet, Massachusetts.

LEO C. IRRERA, Sculptor and Art Coordinator for the Memorial, created the bronze reliefs on the Naval Reserve, Commodore Perry in Japan, and the Seabees—a subject well suited to this Seabee veteran of World War II. Irrera is a sculptor— with a strong background in art history, drawing, painting and photography. He has taught at all levels from elementary to university. He has served as Art Director and Humanities Coordinator for the Newburgh (NY) city schools, and as a communications and media consultant for the New York State Education Department. He has designed and directed special training programs in the private sector, working with foreign personnel, graduate students, faculty and administration. A graduate of the Rhode Island School of Design, he earned his Master of

Fine Arts degree from Indiana University and a postgraduate fellowship in communications and media at Fordham University, there serving as one of the members of Marshall McLuhan's team. This collaboration resulted in the design of the Newburgh Media Project, a major Ford Foundation Grant leading to a working relationship with professionals in the major broadcast networks and in the performing arts. Since resuming his sculpture career, he has produced a number of works in the D.C. area.

EVA AMANN IRRERA, wife of Leo Irrera, designed the title plaques which are mounted above each of the bronze reliefs. Mrs. Irrera is an artist at Northern Virginia Community College.

ROBERT LAMB, sculptor of bronze reliefs on the Navy Family and the U. S. Merchant Marine/ U. S. Navy Armed Guard, was graduated from the Merchant Marine Academy as an engineer. His service in that capacity in World War II enabled him to pursue his real love, art. He studied sculpture at the Rhode Island School of Design and Cornell University, where he earned his Masters, and he later taught for two years at the School of Design. Lamb has exhibited in numerous group and individual shows in New England and New York. Much of his career has been spent in carving stone, although he has worked in a variety of media and is noted for his calligraphy. Furthering his nautical connections, his commissions include the creation for the U. S. government of award trophies bearing the names of Fleet Admiral Chester Nimitz and Admiral Arleigh Burke.

SERENA GOLDSTEIN LITOFSKY, sculpted the bronze reliefs Women in the Navy, and Inland Engagements—the Navy in Vietnam. A native of Charleston, West Virginia, and resident of the Washington metropolitan area since 1969, Litofsky majored in art at the University of California at Los Angeles and received her Master of Fine Arts in Sculpture from American University in Washington. Maintaining a studio in Maryland, she works in stone and plaster as well as clay and wax, all organic materials that she feels are best in constructing natural form. Her works have been shown extensively in the eastern U. S. and are part of many private collections. Of her work on the Women in the Navy bronze relief, she says, "It has been a real pleasure for me to meet and talk with the retired WAVES and current women in the Navy." She adds that her inspiration for the bronze relief came from a visit to a submarine tender in Norfolk that was 40 percent "manned" by women.

ANTONIO TOBIAS MENDEZ, sculptor of the bronze reliefs on Navy Medicine, and Exploration/ Research, was born in Denver and with his family lived for seven years in Okinawa, Japan, and Bangkok, Thailand. In 1974, he came to Maryland where he now resides and maintains his studio. Mendez studied with the Oscar-winning makeup artist and sculptor John Chambers in 1982 and furthered his study of sculpture at the Art Institute of Chicago. Then he was invited to study in Spain with the Spanish sculptor Jose Cobo-Calderon. Both private and corporate commissions fill his portfolio. Besides his participation in the Navy Memorial project, Mendez has been invited by the United States Mint to compete for coin designs commemorating the 50th anniversaries of Mount Rushmore and the USO. Earlier he was commissioned by the United States Park Service for a sculpture for the Pearl Harbor Remembrance Memorial in Oahu, Hawaii.

FRED PRESS, sculptor of the John Paul Jones and U. S. Marine Corps bronze reliefs, is a native of Boston, where he began childhood training in art at the age of six, under the supervision of Boston artist Harold Rotenberg. He received awards and scholarships throughout his childhood, and at the age of 19 co-founded a company which reproduced and sold his original sculptures. Serving in the Army Air Corps in World War II, he was acclaimed for work on a morale boosting magazine published by the Army for service personnel. Following the war he resumed his sculptural activities, quickly distinguishing himself in a succession of shows, exhibits, commissions and competitions. In 1951 he embarked on a career in product development for factories making and marketing wares in a variety of media, with one of Press' designs earning him an award from the Museum of Modern Art in New York. A painter, sculptor and teacher, Press has written numerous magazine and newspaper articles in his field, and he authored *Sculpture at Your Fingertips*. Sculptures from his "Contemporary Collection," created more than 50 years ago, continue to be exhibited in group shows, most recently at the National Arts Club in New York.

KLARA SEVER, sculptor of The Chaplain Corps bronze relief, studied at the School of Art and Design and at the Comenius University in Bratislava, Czechoslovakia. She worked as a sculptor and restorer on some of Czechoslovakia's most beautiful baroque castles and also designed new architectural sculpture for the interior of its National Theater. Since immigrating to the United States, Mrs. Sever has dedicated all of her time to sculpting, exhibiting in a number of galleries in Washington and New York. She has received awards at the National Small Sculpture Competition. Her originals and reproductions can be found in numerous private collections in Europe and the United States. Her bronze relief of one of the founders of the Czechoslovak Republic hangs in the American Embassy in Prague.

MIKLOS SIMON, sculptor of the Naval Academy and Naval Airships bronze reliefs, was born in 1960 in Zalaegerszeg, Hungary. After four years in the Hungarian School of the Arts, he entered his first exhibition with five small sculptures. After a year of additional study at the Academy of Fine Arts in Budapest, he left his homeland for the United States by way of Vienna. Settled in Chicago, he continued his studies at the University of Illinois' Chicago campus and later earned a fine arts degree from the School of the Art Institute of Chicago. Naturalized as a U. S. citizen in 1987, he enrolled the following year in the Master of Fine Arts program at the University of Notre Dame. Taking part in numerous group exhibitions and receiving commissions for the university, he received the competitive Riley Fellowship of a full tuition and stipend. Following exhibits of his thesis work, he returned to Chicago in 1991 to teach a figure-sculpture course at the School of the Art Institute.

ROBERT TEMPLE SUMMERS II, sculptor of the Battle of Mobile Bay, Navy in Space, and the bronze relief honoring the U. S. Coast Guard, was involved in art from his childhood and began painting seriously when he was 24 years old. Working in various media for

The West Sculpture Wall.

painting, he divides his time for "doing bronzes." His creative emphasis has been the American West. He created a life-size, full-figure bronze of a Texas Ranger which is on display at the Texas Ranger Hall of Fame in Waco. Summers was chosen from 100 artists to sculpt a nine foot standing likeness of the late film hero John Wayne. The work is on permanent display at the John Wayne Airport in Orange County, California. Recently he created a three-fourths life-size monument entitled "Texas Legacy," now on permanent display at the Houston Astrodome complex—a gift to the people of Houston from Navy Memorial Foundation Board Chairman Paul N. Howell. Summers has received

numerous awards and honors, including being named by the Texas legislature as the Official Texas Bicentennial Artist.

In addition to these sculptors, including Sculptor and Art Coordinator for the Memorial, Leo Irrera, the Navy Memorial Foundation is indebted to CAPTAIN ROBERT S. JONES, *USN (Ret.),* for his overall management of the bronze relief program—administration, fund raising, liaison with sponsoring organizations, historical research and technical assistance. A native of Kansas City, Missouri, and a journalism graduate of the University of Missouri, Jones enlisted and was later

commissioned in the Navy and served in amphibious operations in the Pacific during World War II. Following the war he became a Navy public affairs specialist, serving in that capacity for 22 years, culminating with duty as Deputy and Acting Director of Defense Information during the Vietnam conflict. After retirement, Captain Jones joined the Navy Memorial Foundation in 1984 to serve five years as Executive Assistant to Foundation president Rear Admiral William Thompson. He played a key role in the planning and design of the Navy Memorial's Visitors Center. For his service with the Foundation, the Secretary of the Navy awarded Captain Jones the Meritorious Public Service Award.

# The Visitors Center

## Education, Heritage Awareness and Remembrance with Art, Technology–and, Sometimes, Tears

### The Quarterdeck

Explaining the parts of ship, a seafaring man (or woman) would tell a landlubber that the *quarterdeck* is the open foyer behind the ship's front door, the main entrance, a spit and polish arena of a neatness reflecting the ship's alert dignity and character. It's not the back porch door to the kitchen. The quarterdeck, the sailor will say, is where the ship greets kings and princes from distant lands, bidding a warm and proud welcome to guests who favor her with a visit.

The Navy Memorial is hardly a ship, but the ship-based equivalent is exactly what is intended in the Quarterdeck of its Visitors Center—whether the kings and princes are from Tibet, Ohio, Utah or Guam.

Immediately the Visitors Center Quarterdeck involves the visitor in America's rich naval heritage starting from its ceiling—the overhead—right down the bulkheads to the deck. A granite frieze recalls the names of great battles, an inlaid gold shorthand—to glorify not the battles but the brave Americans who fought them. Yorktown, Tripoli, Coral Sea, Midway, Guadalcanal, and more—events in which America's crew of Navy people made the difference in American history. The frieze ends with the mention of the Persian Gulf; there is no more room, no space for another name—reflecting a hope and prayer for *no more wars.*

. . . . . . . . . . . . . . . . . . . . . . . . . . . . . . . . . . . . . . . . . . . . . . . . .

### The Wave Wall
### –a Fleet of Two Centuries on a Glass Sea

The Wave Wall incorporates 13 alcoves of glass panels forming an interleaved continuum of three great waves which roll gracefully toward and down into a stairwell vortex to the Gallery Deck. Etched in the glass waves and set in softly illuminated relief are the profiles of 32 ships spanning more than two centuries of American naval history. Half of the etchings are of specific ships and the rest are representative of classes of ships, which understandably cannot take into account various configurations within each class. "Plankowners" and other crewmen of World War II ships and later usually spot the

*At left, the granite frieze and Wave Wall.*

differences in a wink, so the Navy Memorial Foundation wisely begs indulgence for this necessary exercise of artistic license, as it does for all of the other worthy ships and classes that were not included.

Here are the ships depicted or represented on the Wave Wall, starting from the first panel on the right near the Quarterdeck entrance and proceeding to the left and down the staircase:

Panel I

1. *Alfred,* one of the first two merchant ships purchased for the First Continental Fleet, in 1775.
2. *Constitution,* 44 gun frigate, War of 1812.

Panel II

3. *Hartford*-class steam sloop, Civil War.
4. *Monitor,* ironclad, 1862.
5. *Cairo*-class ironclad river steamer, Civil War.

Panel III

6. *Atlanta,* steel cruiser, 1880s.
7. *Brooklyn,* armored cruiser, Spanish American War, 1898.
8. *C-1,* early submarine, 1906.

Panel IV

9. *Wickes*-class flushdeck destroyer, 1920s.
10. *New York*-class battleship, as modernized 1925-27.

**Panel V**

11. *Northampton*-class "treaty" cruiser, 1930s.
12. *Gridley*-class destroyer, 1930s.

**Panel VI**

13. *Lexington*-class aircraft carrier, pre- and World War II.
14. *PC*, pre- and World War II.
15. *"S"*-class sub, pre- and World War II.

**Panel VII**

16. *Commencement Bay*-class escort carrier, World War II.
17. *Cleveland*-class light cruiser, World War II.

**Panel VIII**

18. *Fletcher*-class destroyer, World War II.
19. *LST* (Landing Ship Tank), World War II.

**Panel IX**

20. *Cimarron*-class fleet oiler, World War II.
21. *YMS*, motor minesweeper, World War II.
22. *Gato*-class submarine, World War II.

Wave Wall etching of *USS Arleigh Burke (DDG-51).*

**Panel X**

23. *Essex*-class aircraft carrier, World War II and Korea, before 1950s and 1960s modernization.

24. *Buckley*-class destroyer escort, World War II and Korea.
25. *Long Beach*, first nuclear cruiser, 1960s.
26. *Nautilus*, first nuclear submarine, 1950s.

**Panel XI**

27. *Nimitz*-class nuclear aircraft carrier, 1970s.
28. *Raleigh*-class landing ship dock, 1970s.

**Panel XII**

29. *Iowa*-class battleship, World War II to 1990s.
30. *Ohio*-class Trident ballistic missile submarine, 1980s.

**Panel XIII**

31. *Supply*, fast combat support ship, 1990s.
32. *Arleigh Burke*-class guided missile destroyer, 1990s.

The Visitors Center Quarterdeck, The Homecoming statue and the Wave Wall.

# The Homecoming

## Sailor, Wife and Child Portrayed in Joyous Reunion

Against the broad scope of a granite frieze and the long reach of the Wave Wall stands a focal point for the Quarterdeck, the Homecoming statue, the generous gift of the Fleet Reserve Association.

Navy people aren't the only ones who leave home on business, so the joyous reunion of a sailor, wife and child portrayed in Stanley Bleifeld's Homecoming isn't a new message. But there is more at work here than a quick clinch, the kind seen any Friday night at the airport.

Most business trips don't take six months or more nor do they entail putting lives on the line. So the reunion here evokes a liberation from awesome loneliness and fear—for all the participants. Moreover, as wonderful as the recruiters paint it, the adventure of going to sea is plain hard work and filled with uncertainties—for those who go and those who stay behind. Whole lives have changed during this separation, and great spans of time lost can never be recovered.

This reunion is as much a celebration of success as it is a liberation from hardship. The Homecoming attests to a shared sense of accomplishment, a recognition by sailor, wife and child that each has done the duty set before them. Not only is theirs the triumph of survival, it is a triumph of achievement.

True, there is a romance to going to sea, but The Homecoming reminds us that some of what the swashbucklers brag about is really the romance of coming back home.

Exquisitely capturing the moment shared by two centuries of Navy families, The Homecoming follows the Lone Sailor as Mr. Bleifeld's second major work for the Navy Memorial. The Connecticut-based sculptor developed his design of a Navy family reunion

Stanley Bleifeld's statue, The Homecoming.

after he visited Navy home ports to witness the celebrations for Navy ships and squadrons returning from overseas deployments.

## The Gallery Deck

The Quarterdeck Wave Wall leads the visitor "below decks" to a spacious Gallery Deck—named for a platform at the quarters or around the stern of old-time sailing vessels. The Gallery Deck provides access to The Log Room, the Ship's Store gift shop, interactive videos, the U. S. Presidents Room and a 250-seat motion picture theater.

. . . . . . . . . . . . . . . . . . . . . . . . . . . . . . . . . . . . . . . . . . . . . . . . . . . . . .

## Navy Memorial Log

Preserving the Past,
Building for the Future

The founders of the Navy Memorial created the Navy Memorial Log with a simply stated goal: to be the only place in the world that preserves for public viewing, for all time, the names of Americans who have served in the United States Navy.

The Navy Memorial Log, they reasoned, serves America as no other institution or system is able by recording the name, date and place

of birth, dates of Navy service and highest rate or rank of any person entered in the Log who serves now or who ever served in the Navy. The Log preserves their history in the hallowed setting of a national memorial expressly dedicated to Navy people. The Log underscores the concept of a living memorial—to those who serve or served, whose greatest sacrifice may have been less than the supreme one of giving one's life for one's country.

While those who made supreme and heroic sacrifices are revered here, and while the Log contains names such as John Paul Jones, Stephen Decatur and Chester Nimitz, most are of less well-known Navy people: a proud Navy chief petty officer who entered his own name and that of a son who just completed boot camp and is following in his father's footsteps as a machinist's mate; a pilot who died in World War II and whose name has been entered by his grandchildren; a commanding officer honored by the members of his command on the date of his retirement; a former director of the WAVES; and thousands more men and women of the Navy—from 1775 to the present.

"Even the ravages of wind and rain will not damage this permanent record," said Rear Admiral William Thompson, USN (Ret.), president of the U. S. Navy Memorial Foundation. "Our use of computers makes this a truly modern Memorial, and our Log will last as long as America and its Navy."

Originally designed as a fund raising program, The Log has evolved as part of the enduring, living aspect of the Navy Memorial; it is a constantly renewing record that is never finished, as contributions are received each day on behalf of today's sailors and Navy veterans. From this latter group has come a great outpouring of support for the Navy Memorial, expressed in their generous contributions to a memorial which

Visitor Center staffer Commander John Hoshko and watchstander Claire L. Dunn await visitors to the Navy Memorial Log Room.

Congress authorized but did not fund. As the Navy Memorial approached the mid-1990s, nearly 200,000 Navy veterans and their active duty shipmates or their adoring families had contributed $25 or more to record their names and service information in the Log and help complete construction of the Memorial.

Before the dedication of the Navy Memorial in 1987 and as the last sections were being placed in the granite map of the world, Rear Admiral Thompson placed a computer tape cassette record of the Log as is was thus far compiled under the stone section immediately to the right of the Great Lakes region— symbolically making the Log a permanent part of the Memorial's stonework.

All who donated to the Navy Memorial or enrolled in the Navy Memorial Log before the opening of the Visitors Center received blue plastic "Plankowner" cards, embossed with the donor's or enrollee's name, attesting to his or her founding stake in the Memorial—a carryover from the Navy tradition that a ship's first

crew are its "plankowners." Since the opening of the Visitors Center, new donors to the Navy Memorial and enrollees in the Log receive a white plastic "Shipmate" card.

In 1989, the Navy Memorial Foundation added a new opportunity for history-conscious Navy people: they may add a

. . . . . . . . . . . . . . .

*"Our use of computers makes this a truly modern memorial, and our Log will last as long as America and its Navy."*

. . . . . . . . . . . . . . .

photograph to their Log record, or enter the Log information and photograph all at the same time. The Navy Memorial Foundation selected Eastman Kodak to implement the program to include a photograph as part of each Log entry. Eastman Kodak set up a similar program for the centennial of the Statue of Liberty. The system integrates photos and Log text electronically, so that both can be displayed on a video screen or printed out for visitors to take home with them.

The Log is on permanent display in the Log Room located off the Visitors Center's Gallery Deck. The Log is scrolled continuously on large video displays, and visitors may access any one of the video terminals where they may view the Log enrollment of themselves, friends or loved ones who served in the Navy. Visitors may order printouts of the Log information and pay for them in the Ship's Store which adjoins the Log Room.

"Throughout this Navy Memorial project, we have constantly sought ways to make this truly a memorial dedicated to the individual men and women who have made the U. S. Navy great," said Stevii Graves, the first coordinator of the Log. "Now, instead of just reading about Log entrants, generations to come will be able to see the faces of everyday Navy people and fully appreciate the human dimension of our Navy's history."

*How to Enroll in the Navy Memorial Log*

If you or a loved one serves or has served in the Navy and you would like to enroll in the Navy Memorial Log, send to the address below the entrant's full name, date and place of birth, inclusive dates of naval service and highest rate or rank attained. You may also send a photograph of the entrant. Photos may be any size up to 8-inches by 10-inches, in black and white or color. Only one photo will be included in a Log entry. The Foundation recommends that an individual shot be provided; if a group shot is all that is available, the Log member in the group should be indicated so the curator of the Log can crop a close-up view of the Log member. To date, most people have chosen to include a photo taken during the period of the Log member's naval service. *None of the photos submitted will be returned.*

The "cost" to add a photograph to an existing Log entry is $25, and a new Log entry with a photo is $50. Log entries without photographs will continue to require a minimum donation of $25. Log enrollment contributions are fully tax deductible. Check or money order payable to "U. S. Navy Memorial" may be mailed along with Log information and photograph to:

U. S. Navy Memorial
    Foundation
P. O. Box 96570
Washington, DC 20090-6570

Contributions may also be made by MasterCard or Visa, by mail to the above address; include account number, expiration date and exact name of cardholder appearing on the card. Log enrollments may also be made in person at the Visitors Center. Please note: It is important to understand the distinction between donors to the Navy Memorial and enrollees in the Navy Memorial Log; only naval service active duty personnel or veterans, living or dead, are eligible for enrollment in the Navy Memorial Log. But anyone may donate to the Navy Memorial as much and as often as he or she desires.

# A Fantastic Ship's Store

One of the most fascinating new shopping stops on Pennsylvania Avenue is the Ship's Store in the Visitors Center. The store offers jewelry, books for children and adults, apparel, games, models, toys, prints and posters, flag cases, maps and charts and globes—all of it relating in some way to the Navy Memorial.

Among the best sellers in the store are printouts of entries in the Navy Memorial Log (located next door to the store), prints of ships and aircraft displayed on the interactive video kiosks on the Gallery Deck, bonded bronze replicas of the Lone Sailor and Homecoming statues, "Plankowner" ball caps and assorted Memorial tee shirts.

The Ship's Store is open for business whenever the Visitors Center is open to the general public.

*The only shop of its kind in the nation's capital, the Ship's Store is a nautical delight, filled with seagoing treasures sought by discriminating mariner-adventurers down through the ages.*

# U. S. Presidents Room

The U. S. Presidents Room pays tribute to American Presidents who served in the naval establishment. The U. S. Presidents Room accommodates a wide variety of meetings and may be rented to groups at commercial rates. The facility has been outfitted with a full-service pantry to support catering service. Groups using the room will have access to state-of-the-art audio-visual equipment, including teleconferencing.

Who are the "Navy's Presidents?" Technically, all of America's Presidents qualify, serving as they do as Commander-in-Chief of the armed forces. But among them all is a select group of eight Presidents who are uniquely "Navy." Theodore Roosevelt and Franklin D. Roosevelt served as Assistant Secretaries of the Navy. Presidents serving in Navy uniform include John F. Kennedy, Lyndon Johnson, Richard Nixon, Gerald Ford, Jimmy Carter and George Bush. All are honored in the U. S. Presidents room with their portraits showing them at the time of their service with the Navy. The portraits were rendered by art students in the Washington area who successfully competed for the opportunity to have their works displayed in the U. S. Presidents Room.

### THEODORE ROOSEVELT—*26th President, 1901-1909*

Appointed Assistant Secretary of the Navy by President William McKinley, Theodore Roosevelt took office on April 19, 1897, and served almost exactly one year. Roosevelt overshadowed the incumbent Secretary of the Navy through his outspoken advocacy for a rapid buildup of the Navy. At the outbreak of the Spanish American War in April 1898. Roosevelt accepted appointment as a lieutenant colonel, second in command of the First U. S. Volunteer Cavalry—his famed "Rough Riders." Later, as President, Roosevelt deployed a U. S. Navy "Great White Fleet" in a combined goodwill and show of force round-the-world voyage.

IRWIN BAUM, *Artist*
New Rochelle, New York
Graduate student, The George Washington University

### FRANKLIN DELANO ROOSEVELT—*32nd President, 1933-1945*

President Woodrow Wilson appointed Franklin D. Roosevelt Assistant Secretary of the Navy, a post he held from 1913 to 1920, encompassing the years of World War I. Following in his cousin Theodore's footsteps, FDR focused on the Navy's preparedness for the approaching war. Civilian personnel, Navy yards and docks and the purchase of supplies were in his purview, and he made significant improvements in productivity and procurement. He fought hard for antisubmarine warfare systems to help break the German U-boat threat in the Atlantic.

FRANK A. DEMES, *Artist*
Newburgh, New York
Graduate student, The George Washington University

### JOHN FITZGERALD KENNEDY—*35th President, 1961-1963*

John F. Kennedy entered the Navy in September 1941, three months before the Japanese attack on Pearl Harbor. He received a commission and in late 1942 was assigned to a motor torpedo boat squadron where he took command of his boat, *PT-109*. On the night of August 2, 1943, Kennedy's boat was rammed and cut in half by a Japanese destroyer. Although badly injured in his back, after 15 hours in the water he led his surviving crewmen to a small island. Kennedy was awarded the Navy and Marine Corps Medal. After hospitalization in the U. S., Kennedy served as an instructor before his discharge in March 1945.

SANDRA REED, *Artist*
Washington, Iowa
Graduate student, The George Washington University

### LYNDON BAINES JOHNSON—*36th President, 1963-1969*

Lyndon Johnson was a member of Congress at the outbreak of World War II and also a member of the Naval Reserve. Volunteering for active service, he was appointed a lieutenant commander in the Navy. He was the first Congressman to don a uniform in the war, where he served as President Roosevelt's special emissary in Australia and New Zealand. Johnson was decorated with the Silver Star for gallantry under fire when a patrol bomber in which he was flying as an observer came under enemy attack. His active naval career ended when President Roosevelt ruled that legislators might not serve in the armed forces.

KEBEDECH TEKLEAB, *Artist*
Addis Ababa, Ethiopia
Senior at Howard University

RICHARD MILHOUS NIXON—*37th President, 1969-1974*

Richard Nixon left a successful law practice in Whittier, California, to take part in the war effort. He went to Washington and a job doing legal work in the Office of Price Administration, but after a few months he decided help out more directly in the war effort—despite his Quaker background. He entered the Navy in August 1942, appointed as a lieutenant junior grade. He was sent to the South Pacific and served as a ground officer for the Combat Air Transport Command on Bougainville, Vella Lavella and Green Islands. After 15 months and two battle stars, Nixon returned to shore duty in the U. S. He was discharged in the rank of lieutenant commander in January 1946.

> TRINKA SIMON, *Artist*
> Cordamedera, California
> Master of Fine Arts, American University

GERALD R. FORD—*38th President, 1974-1977*

Gerald Ford joined the Navy in April 1942. A star athlete at the University of Michigan, he was assigned to provide physical training for V-5 program aviation cadets at the University of North Carolina. Longing to see action in the war, Ford requested transfer to Norfolk, Virginia, for gunnery training; he was then assigned to duty in the aircraft carrier *USS Monterey* as the director of physical education and assistant navigation officer. *USS Monterey* operated with the Third and Fifth Fleets in the Pacific and, in the final year of heavy fighting, participated in almost every major naval engagement of the South Pacific, earning Ford ten battle stars. Ford later served with the Naval Air Training Program until his discharge in January 1946 as a lieutenant commander.

> PABLO RAMELLA, *Artist*
> Buenos Aires, Argentina
> Junior at The George Washington University

JAMES EARL CARTER, JR.—*39th President, 1977-1981*

Jimmy Carter entered the U. S. Naval Academy in Annapolis in 1943 and in a wartime accelerated course graduated with distinction in 1946. Carter served in surface ships operating out of Norfolk and then volunteered for submarine duty. After serving in *USS Pomfret (SS-391)*, Carter joined the commissioning crew of *USS Barracuda (SSK-1)*, rising to the position of executive officer. Qualified for command in 1952 and promoted to lieutenant, Carter entered the Navy's nuclear power program and was the senior officer in the pre-commissioning crew of the *USS Seawolf*, one of the Navy's first nuclear powered submarines, and worked under direct supervision of Captain Hyman G. Rickover. After the death of his father, Carter resigned from the Navy in 1953 to run the family's business.

> LINDA STANIER, *Artist*
> Bowie, Maryland
> Graduate student, The George Washington University

GEORGE HERBERT WALKER BUSH—*41st President, 1989-*

In 1942 George Bush enlisted in the Naval Reserve and entered flight training at Naval Air Station Corpus Christi, Texas. Commissioned an ensign, in late 1943 he joined VT-51, Torpedo Bomber Squadron 51, embarked in the light aircraft carrier *USS San Jacinto*. For awhile the youngest pilot in the Navy, he was shot down near Chichi Jima in the Bonin Islands and was rescued by submarine *USS Finback*. As a combat pilot he earned the Distinguished Flying Cross and three Air Medals. After rotation home in 1944, he trained new pilots in Virginia Beach, Virginia, before his discharge as a lieutenant junior grade in 1945.

> ROBERT LIBERACE, *Artist*
> Monsey, New York
> Graduate student, The George Washington University

# AT SEA

### There is no other journey like it.

The majesty...the challenge...
powerfully revealed in the vision and sound
of the Super Horizon 70 Screen

**United States Navy Memorial**
**Pennsylvania Avenue, N.W.**
**Between 7th & 9th Streets**
**Washington, D.C.**
**Metro's Archives/Navy Memorial Station**

**Visitors Center**
**10AM-6PM Monday-Saturday**
**Noon-5PM Sunday**
**Screenings every 45 minutes**

**A MacGillivray Freeman Film**

**Made possible by Mobil**

# Arleigh and Roberta Burke Theater

The Arleigh and Roberta Burke Theater is Washington's newest and possibly most exciting facility designed from the ground up to exhibit high-resolution 70mm motion picture productions.

The theater is named for the beloved and legendary war hero and three-term Chief of Naval Operations, Admiral Arleigh A. Burke, and his wife Roberta. Having breathed life into the idea of a modern Navy Memorial, Admiral Burke is truly considered one of its founders. In an illustrious career shared by a dedicated husband and wife team, Admiral and Mrs. Burke have touched the lives of untold thousands of men and women of the Navy—and their families.

Located in the Visitors Center, the Burke Theater showcases the MacGillivray Freeman Films' 70 millimeter experiential motion picture spectacular *At Sea*. The theater "floats"—suspended within the space of two stories in Market Square East, a 13-story, mixed-use commercial and residential building. To support the weight of the theater within the host building, the foundation floor received extra concrete-and-steel reinforcement. With bell cranks imbedded on its underside, a floating slab forming the theater's floor was poured above the reinforced slab, separated by a one inch air space. The ceiling is three-layered, one attached to the underside of the upper floor, a middle layer suspended from sound isolating hangers, and the lowest level suspended from the middle one. The walls are isolated from the rest of the building with layers of neoprene and are covered with acoustically wrapped panels.

Morris Architects designed the facility to provide excellent acoustics, to keep outside sounds from entering the theater, and to contain and isolate sound from the rest of the building. Containing the sound is the greater task: nothing else in the vicinity—not even the Metro subway system several floors below—can match the output of the Burke Theater's powerful six-track digital surround sound system. The state-of-the-art JBL audio system is capable of delivering up to 4200 watts, bi-amplified, through five discrete full-range channels—three behind the screen and one in each side wall for left and right surround sound—and one discrete sub-woofer system housed in two cabinets, also behind the screen.

The theater's 70mm film

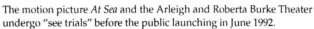

The motion picture *At Sea* and the Arleigh and Roberta Burke Theater undergo "see trials" before the public launching in June 1992.

The Arleigh and Roberta Burke Theater features a curved screen two-stories high by 52 feet wide, and seats 241 people.

projector is equipped with a custom-ground 45mm lens to project the largest possible frame image on the theater's two-story by 52-foot screen. As fast as the original footage ran through MacGillivray Freeman cameras, the final film print passes through the projector at 30 frames per second vice the normal 24 frames per second—a 25 percent faster rate than conventional camera-projection equipment. This greater speed adds to the brilliance and clarity of the film and makes rapid movements on the screen appear smoother and more realistic. The film is stored and driven through dust-free film cabinets containing an elaborate arrangement of rollers which keep the film from touching itself and possibly harming the emulsion. A single print of a movie can last ten times longer than possible with conventional reel or platter storage systems. Iwerks Entertainment, Burbank, California, designed the projection and audio systems. A world leader in custom, special-venue motion picture theater design, the firm was founded by Don Iwerks, creator of projection systems used by the Disney organization.

The arrangement of the theater's 241 seats with handicapped accommodations for up to nine patrons provides a high ratio of image-to-viewer distance, an important factor in the visual impact of a film presentation. The ratio for the Burke Theater is among the highest of theaters in the Washington area. The theater program is completely automated requiring only one person to start

Theater queing area, designed and furnished by Eastman Kodak.

the controls which open the doors, dim the lights, open the curtain, start the movie and reverse the process at the end of the program.

The theater's seats have been sponsored by donations of $1,000 or more for each seat—another opportunity for patrons to support the Memorial. Each sponsored theater seat has a brass plate imbedded in its solid wood arm, inscribed with the name of a ship, squadron, unit or individual to be commemorated.

Like the U. S. Presidents Room, the theater is available for rental for private functions such as board meetings, presentations, conventions, etc.. A wide variety of film, video and other audio visual formats can be supported, including full-color computer projection, slides, 16mm and 35mm motion pictures, live television (via cable) and video tape projection and overhead projections.

. . . . . . . . . . . . . . . . . .

**The United States Navy Memorial presents**

**The exciting vision and experience of the sea in a great motion picture presentation in the Arleigh and Roberta Burke Theater**

*"It's incredibly exhilarating and deeply satisfying to be a part of it all. It gives your life a particular meaning; you're not just punching a clock. . . Somewhere in the back of your brain, you always know that it won't be long before you're back out at sea."*

. . . . . . . . . . . . . . . . . .

Producer/Writer Alec Lorimore, Producer/Director Greg MacGillivray and Cameraman Brad Ohlund prepare to shoot a scene for the United States Navy Memorial film, *At Sea.* Created for exclusive exhibition at the Navy Memorial, the 70mm film is projected onto a unique Super Horizon 70 screen. The engulfing film experience puts the audience on the flight deck of an aircraft carrier, in the cockpit of an F-14, and aboard other Navy vessels to document the drama of life at sea.

Spoken about the sea, this comment by one Navy man in the film *At Sea* might well apply to the film itself. For many who see it, it won't be long before they're back to see it again. Underwritten by Mobil Corporation, *At Sea* gives the viewers the "incredibly exhilarating and deeply satisfying experience" of going to sea in Navy ships.

Showing exclusively in The Burke Theater, the 35-minute "experiential" presentation is the creation of MacGillivray Freeman Films of Laguna Beach, California. The firm also produced the widely-acclaimed *To Fly*, seen at the National Air and Space Museum since 1976.

*At Sea* tells its story through the eyes, words and actions of an active duty naval officer, Lieutenant Ray Turner. The camera follows Turner as he leaves his family to go to sea in the aircraft carrier *USS Constellation.* Turner is a catapult launch officer, a key figure in the high-pitched, high-pressure action that takes place during flight operations. Through his eyes, we see the commitment to mission that binds his team together. With close looks at what it takes to load, launch and land the jets on the flight deck in all weather, we come to understand what makes these men such a close-knit, efficient and effective team. We see how the

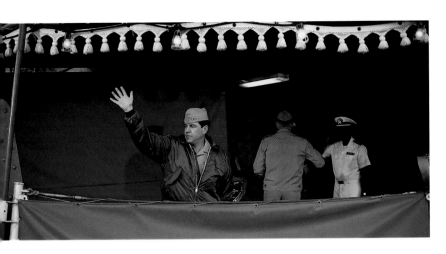

# AT SEA

**There is no other journey like it.**

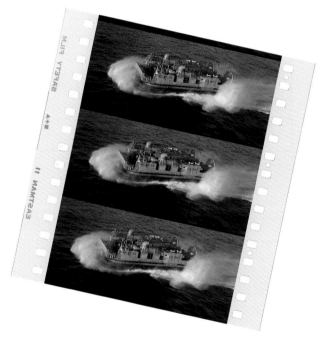

*Scenes from the dedication of the Arleigh and Roberta Burke Theater and premiere of the film* At Sea, *June 12, 1992.*

training shapes youth into professionals and teaches the value of cooperation. We see how people work together to accomplish a mission. And we experience the intensity and excitement of what it is like to be at sea on one of the largest vessels ever built.

Add to this exciting story the method of its telling, a film format that is unique in Washington. Many large-format productions are filmed in 35-millimeter stock and then enlarged to 70-millimeters; *At Sea* was filmed, beginning to end, in 70-millimeters. To match the Burke Theater's projection system noted earlier, MacGillivray Freeman's cameras voraciously consumed film at a 25 percent faster rate than conventional equipment.

All the artistic and technology features of the film and its presentation combine to reveal the majesty and power of the oceans— and of the American sailors who are the film's cast in a day-in, day-out drama at sea. Set in a modern context, the film is like all the major features of the Navy Memorial and the Visitors Center; it represents and pays tribute to generations of Navy people—past, present and future.

Film and television star Tom Selleck, center, cuts the ribbon—a strip of 70mm film—opening the Arleigh and Roberta Burke Theater. Also pictured, left to right, Anthony R. Corso, Mobil Corporation; Washington, D.C. Councilwoman Charlene Drew Jarvis; Under Secretary of the Navy J. Daniel Howard; Rear Admiral Thompson.

NAVY MEMORIAL ★ VISITORS CENTER

NAVY
MEMORI
VISITO
C

FOR | THOSE IN PERIL ON THE SEA |

One of the Memorial's two ship masts
bids welcome to visitors.

A horn of plenty—of music—performs in a
"Concert on the Avenue" at the Memorial.

These crew members of *USS Kitty Hawk (CV-63)* are among the millions of men and
women of the Navy, past and present, who are honored by the Navy Memorial.

# U.S. Navy Memorial's Fleet of Major Contributors

The U. S. Navy Memorial is being funded from enrollments in the Navy Memorial Log, other individual gifts, sponsorships of Memorial and Visitor Center furnishings and larger contributions from the Memorial's Fleet of Major Contributors. The names of Log entrants are forever inscribed in the Log itself. The Fleet of Major Contributors is listed here and also in a lighted display panel on the Quarterdeck wall, adjacent to the elevator. This powerful (and generous) fleet continues to grow, and succeeding editions of this book will add the names of new corporate and individual donors. The Navy Memorial Foundation appreciates the outstanding support received from the following organizations and individuals:

## Fleet Commanders in Chief
(more than $500,000)

Mobil Corporation
  more than Two Million Dollars
Fleet Reserve Association
  more than One Million Dollars
Forrest E. Mars, Sr.
  One Million Dollars

## Fleet Commanders
(more than $250,000)

Grumman Corporation

## Task Force Commanders
(more than $200,000)

Boeing Company
General Dynamics Corporation
General Electric Company
Lockheed Corporation

## Task Group Commanders
($150,000 to $200,000)

Japanese Maritime Self-Defense Force
  and Civilian Volunteers
Martin Marietta Corporation
McDonnell Douglas Corporation
Rockwell International
Texaco Inc.
Unisys Corporation

## Flotilla Commanders
($100,000 to $150,000)

Government of Argentina
Government of Australia
Republic of China

Eastman Kodak Company
  Federal Government Markets
Government of France
William Randolph Hearst Foundation
Republic of Korea
Jacksonville Navy Memorial
  Foundation, Inc.
Raytheon Company
Government of Spain
United Technologies Corporation

## Squadron Commanders
($50,000 to $100,000)

Association of Naval Aviation
Avenue Associates, Trammell
  Crow Company, Dutch Institutional
  Holding Company
Babcock & Wilcox Company
Mrs. Robert Crown
COMPAQ
Destroyer Escort Sailors Association
Federal Republic of Germany
General Motors Corporation
Goodyear Tire and Rubber Company
Gould Inc.
Hughes Aircraft Company
GMC John Kopach
Ladies Auxiliary of the FRA
Robert E. Naser
Naval Airship Association
Navy Supply Corps Association
Newport News Shipbuilding
Past and present . . .
  Naval Reservists
  Navy Chaplains
  Navy Medical Personnel
  Seabees
  U.S. Marines
  Women in the Navy
Naval Academy Alumni Association
Submarine Veterans of World War II
System Planning Corporation
Textron

## Division Commanders
($25,000 to $50,000)

Allied-Signal Inc.
Bloedorn Foundation
British Aerospace, Inc.
Eaton Corporation
Mr. and Mrs. Zachary Fisher
Kirby Foundation
Naval Order of the U. S.
Norfolk Southern Corporation
Northrop Corporation
Quadrangle Development Corporation
Sanders Associates, Inc.
W. M. Schlosser Company
U. S. Coast Guard personnel
U. S. LST Association
U. S. Naval Institute Foundation

## Unit Commanders
($10,000 to $25,000)

AFL-CIO
Amerada Hess Corporation
American Electric Power Company
American Express Company
American Petroleum Institute
Ashland Oil Foundation
Bath Iron Works
Brown Foundation, Inc.
Mr. and Mrs. C. Thomas Clagett, Jr.
Crestar Bank N. A.
D.C. Council, Navy League of the U. S.
Emerson Electric Company
E-Systems, Inc.
FMC Corporation
Freed Foundation
Mrs. Mary Hoffman
RADM and Mrs. Paul N. Howell
Howell Corporation
Howell Foundation
Grand Hyatt at Washington Center
S. Steven Karalekas
Kirkpatrick Foundation, Inc.
Litton Industries
The Melara Club of Italy
RADM and Mrs. William Narva
Patrol Craft Sailors Association
RCA Corporation
CAPT Samuel Wm. Sax
Scientific Management
  Associates, Inc.
Shell Companies Foundation
Tesoro Petroleum Corporation
Texas Instruments
TRW, Inc.
Pacific Northwest WAVES.
Whitehead Foundation

## Ship Captains
($5,000 to $10,000)

Allied Bendix Aerospace
American Hospital Association
American Medical Association
ANA Washington-Anacostia Squadron
Archer Daniels Midland Company
Arthur Andersen & Company
Mr. and Mrs. Gene Autry
Frank E. Basil, Inc.
Barber Construction Corporation
Battle Group Delta
Warren S. Bellows, Jr.
Berlin Publications, Inc.
Bird-Johnson Company
Henry P. Boisvert III
Booz Allen & Hamilton, Inc.
Broward (FL) Council, Navy League
William Julius Breuer
Capital City Br. 67, Fleet Reserve Assn.
CAPT and Mrs. Gordon H. Clow

Navy Memorial Foundation officials participating in the May 1984 groundbreaking include, from left, Captain Samuel Wm. Sax, USNR; Captain William S. Norman, USNR; former Master Chief Petty Officer of the Navy Delbert Black; former Secretaries of the Navy W. Graham Claytor, Jr., and Edward Hidalgo; Ann Wood Farmer; Admiral George E. R. Kinnear II, USN (Ret.); William A. Leonard; Mrs. Robert Crown; Captain S. Steven Karalekas, USNR; and Rear Admiral William Thompson, USN (Ret.), president of the U. S. Navy Memorial Foundation.

City of America
Colt Industries Inc.
Control Data Corporation
Cubic Corporation
Delaware Investment Association
Delex Corporation
Diagnostic/Retrieval Systems, Inc.
BMC Vasily Domoretsky
DynCorp
Evaluation Research Corporation
Fansteel/Custom Technologies Corporation
Mrs. Arthur M. Faggart
Paul Fay
Federal Data Corporation
Mr. and Mrs. Gordon Felder
Figgie International
Fleishman Hillard, Inc.
Robert W. Galvin
GEICO
Gibbs & Cox, Inc.
LCDR and Mrs. Fred B. Glover
Grabill Corporation
GMMC Charles J. Hajcsisak
Mr. and Mrs. Warren O. Hilton
Indal Limited
International Brotherhood of Electrical Workers
Kaman Corporation

Kohler Company
Kollsman Instrument Company
Kretschmar Brands, Inc.
A. Dix Leeson
Maersk Line, Limited
Metropolitan Life Insurance Company
National Softdrink Association/ Coca-Cola Enterprises North
National Steel and Shipbuilding Co.
Naval Air Facility, Atsugi, Japan
Navistar
Mr. and Mrs. Phillip G. Norton
ORI Group
Pagliaro Brothers Stone Company, Inc.
B. Waring Partridge III
PEPSI-CO
Peterson Builders, Inc.
Philip Morris Companies, Inc.
Walter F. Philipp
Thomas G. Pownall
Mrs. W. C. Reeder
Mrs. Eugene Henry Rietzke
Rolls-Royce Inc.
CDR John F. Schneider, Jr.
Sachs/Freeman Associates, Inc.
Adolph Schoepe
Seafarers International Union
G.D. Searle & Company

Sippican, Inc.
Sony Corporation of America
Spartan Corporation
Mr. and Mrs. Roger Staubach
Marvin Stone
Syscon Corporation
CDR Allyn Rhonda Thompson
RADM and Mrs. William Thompson
Todd Shipyards, Inc.
United Services Life Insurance Company
United States Historical Society
USA Today
U. S. Coast Guard Chief Petty Officers Association
USS Indiana Reunion Association
USS St. Louis Association
Vantage Travel Service, Inc.
Veda International, Inc.
Virginia Power Company
Vitro Corporation
VSE Corporation
Waste Management, Inc.
Williams International
The Abe Wouk Foundation
Xerox Corporation
CDR Otto Zipf

September 1992

The U. S. Navy Memorial Foundation appreciates the outstanding support
received from these organizations and individuals.

# United States Navy Memorial Foundation Board of Directors

# U. S. Navy Memorial Foundation Staff

*President*
Rear Admiral William Thompson,
  USN (Ret.)

*Executive Director*
Captain Howard H. Loving, Jr.,
  USN (Ret.)

*Director of the Navy Memorial*
  *and Visitors Center*
Commander James J. Nemer,
  USN (Ret.)

*Master Chief of the Navy Memorial*
Master Chief Hospital Corpsman
  Jay Hood, USN (Ret.)

Marilyn N. Baker
Captain Thomas Coldwell,
  USN (Ret.)
Vickie R. Davis
Senior Chief Hospital Corpsman
  Donald J. Dupuis, USN (Ret.)
James R. Fleckenstein, CAE
Commander Ralph F. Freese,
  SC, USN (Ret.)
Trianne Freese
Paul T. Haley
Commander John Hoshko,
  USN (Ret.)
Master Chief Navy Counselor
  Dave J. Michael, Jr., USN (Ret.)
Patrick M. Pacak
Renato R. Pascual
Rita Robertson
Emmon S. Rogers

Elisabeth J. Saunier
Althea D. Turner

*Log Room Watchstanders*
Claire L. Dunn
Navy Counselor First Class
  Prentice E. Godley, USN (Ret.)
Rose Marie Lawing
Nan B. McComber
Mary J. O'Connor
Maryann P. O'Donnell
Merrill S. Quast
Rosemary P. Schoultz

*Ship's Store Storekeepers*
Edward V. Mikesell
Rebecca L. Roesch
William E. Wort

• • • • • • • • • • • • • • •

# Project Officer

The Foundation extends special thanks to a member of its staff, James J. Nemer, for his outstanding service as project officer for the construction of the Memorial and for the design and construction of the Visitors Center.

Drawing on his artistic and managerial abilities and on his great interest in architecture and design, Jim Nemer has ably served the Memorial since his retirement from the Navy in 1985. A native of Omaha, Nebraska, Jim served in surface ships before becoming a public affairs specialist for assignments ashore and afloat in the U. S. and abroad. Rising to the rank of Commander, he concluded his active service as public affairs officer for the Office of Naval Research. He serves now as Director of the Navy Memorial and the Visitors Center.

• • • • • • • • • • • • • • •

# Where Credit Is Due

The Board of Directors and Staff of the U. S. Navy Memorial Foundation are indebted to many individuals and companies that have contributed to the overall success of the planning and construction of the Navy Memorial and the Visitors Center. We thank each of them for their support and express special appreciation to:

Adame Custom Creations
American Iron Inc.
APPCO Inc.
Avenue Associates Limited
    Partnership
B & B Caterers
Baker Videoactive
Baker Mediasource
Barber Construction Corporation
Brady & Anglin Consulting
    Engineers
Business Furniture and Interiors
Celtic Demolition Co.
Central Armature Works
Columbia Welders and Iron
    Works, Inc.
Columbia Gardens Memorials
Columbian Woodworking Co.
Commercial Glass Studios

Commission of Fine Arts
COMPAQ Computers
Conklin Rossant Architects
Cornell A.E.C.
Trammell Crow Co.
Dahlgren Division, Naval Sea
    Cadets
Defense Mapping Service
Delano Demolition
Delta Group
Denaults Commercial Carpet
Department of the Navy
Department of the Interior
Design Link
Dixon Products
Dynalectric Co., Inc.
Eastman Kodak
Eureka Van and Storage Co., Inc.
The Eichner Group, Inc.
Gilbane Building Co.
Ginns
Haynes Whaley Associates
B. E. Higgs Co.
Hudson Shatz Mid-Atlantic
    Painting Co., Inc.
InVision Communications, Inc.
Iwerks Entertainment
Paul R. Jackson Construction Co.
Jaffe, Inc.
JG Furniture

C. M. Kling & Associates, Inc.
Maryland Sound
McGillivray Freeman Productions
Morris Architects
National Archives
National Capital Planning
    Commission
National Park Service
National Capital Flag Co., Inc.
New England Stone Industries, Inc.
Overhead Door Co. of Washington,
    Inc.
P & P Drywall
Pagliaro Brothers Stone Co.
Pennsylvania Avenue Development
    Corp.
Pran, Inc.
Quality Masonry
W. M. Schlosser Co., Inc.
Security, Inc.
Service Glass Co.
Jack Stone Sign Co.
Stretchwall Products Co., Inc.
Texel Corp.
Triangle Fire Protection
Troiano Tile and Marble
Truland Electric
Washington Woodworking Co.
Wheaton Van Lines, Inc.

. . . . . . . . . . . . . . . . . . . . . . . . . . . . . . . . . . . . . . . . . . . . . . . . . . . . . . . . . . . . . . . . . . . . . .

## Photo Credits

Captain Thomas Coldwell
    13, 18, 19, top 21, statue 22, 27, 28, 35,
    91, middle 93, top 98, 104, top left 105
Paul Davis Studios
    Painting 96
Bill Fitz-Patrick
    86, 88, 89, 93, bottom 102, 103
PHC John Frankavello
    53
Harold J. Gerwien
    12, 14, bottom 21, 45, 56, 76,
    top right 105, 112
James Hawkins
    Bottom 93
Captain Robert S. Jones
    6, 20, left 26, 50, 58, 73, 80, 85

MacGillivray Freeman Films
    99, 100, 101
Ernest McIver
    Cover 1, 82
Mobil Corporation
    Top 102
PH1 Chuck Mussi
    13, 17
National Capital Planning Commission
    5
James J. Nemer
    9, 16, 23, right 26, 109
James Parker
    90, 92, 94, 95, 97, bottom 98
PA1 Dave Santos
    68

PH3 Mark C. Shaffer
    Bottom 105
U.S. Marine Corps
    67
U.S. Navy
    11, 39, 40, 46, 49, 55, 61, 63, 64, 71, 74,
    79, 107
PH2 Van S. West
    64
Rolland White
    38, 41, 43, 44, 47, 48, 51, 53, 54, 57, 59, 60,
    62, 65, 66, 69, 70, 72, 75, 77, 78, 81
PH1 W.H. Williams, Jr.
    42
Brian R. Wolff
    15, flag 22, top 88, top 92, 111

# When the Paper Was Blank

REAR ADMIRAL WILLIAM THOMPSON, President of the Navy Memorial Foundation, penned the official welcome message which appears at the front of this guide. Alongside is an "official" biography, the one the Foundation hands out to reporters. But there's more.

Bill Thompson is the Foundation's first executive director and president. He started without pay steering the Foundation through each step of a long, hard journey—legislation, design, site selection, fund raising and construction. He worked with all the players, the Congress, three Administrations, the District of Columbia, architects, sculptors, contractors, contributors and a succession of Foundation directors.

He started when the paper was blank, when all that existed was a long and widely held desire for a Navy Memorial. Never mind the first design for the Memorial was rejected. Bill Thompson started anew on a concept "in house," which design is what you see today. He kept himself focused, devising workable concepts, plans and actions to reach results—the Navy Memorial and the Visitors Center.

Bill Thompson took up the hard job: He led a deserving charitable cause but one which cures no illness, feeds or shelters no one, memorializes no war nor solely those who died (heroically or not) in the line of duty. Against these limitations, he performed the difficult task of marshaling public and private support for this living Memorial.

Rear Admiral Thompson has never lost his vision or faith in a Navy Memorial. And while he has performed a practical service by helping bring life back to America's Main Street, Pennsylvania Avenue, his most enduring achievement has been to create this simple and eloquent national monument, a living tribute to the people of the Navy.

In making this come to pass, Bill Thompson has further enriched America's naval and maritime heritage.

—TC